RACQUETBALL:
THE CULT

Eugene L. Scott

Introduction by Charlie Brumfield

DOLPHIN BOOKS

DOUBLEDAY & COMPANY, INC., GARDEN CITY, NEW YORK

1979

Also by Eugene L. Scott
TENNIS: GAME OF MOTION

DESIGNED BY MARILYN SCHULMAN

A Dolphin Book
Doubleday & Company, Inc.

Library of Congress Cataloging in Publication Data

Scott, Eugene, 1937–
  Racquetball, the cult.

  1. Racquetball—History.   I. Title.
GV1017.R3S37   796.3′4
ISBN: 0-385-13006-6
Library of Congress Catalog Card Number 77–75883

Acknowledgments

The author's mind was a blank tablet on racquetball. I not only couldn't play—or even keep score—I didn't know how to spectate. Nothing. Yet my experience is what thousands of weekend athletes face in taking up racquetball for the first time.

There were many people who accelerated that experience for me. And made it incredibly exciting as well. I will name them all in no particular sequence—not even alphabetical.

Robert Kendler, the NRC's boss man, was not only helpful, he was so enthusiastic about everything he discussed that he fired up my own motivations for the book project. A book could be and should be written about his own accomplishments and his spirit. Bob's assistant, Chuck Leve, was co-operative and understanding in my George Plimpton-type bumbling during my first tournament efforts.

Charlie Drake of Leach Industries spent time with me that he didn't have. Top pro Steve Strandemo spent time that he did have. Steve is one of the few in racquetball who is struggling. Part of this is because he has chosen to be a maverick and not align with any of the obvious power factors in the sport, and partly because his maverick status has made him aware—while others are not—that projecting a new sport to major status is a struggle, not just a dream.

Arthur Shay, who provided some of the photographs, is an integral part of the racquetball fraternity. Art Seitz, who contributed some graphic-action shots, is like myself a newcomer to racquetball.

Tom McKie, the former IRA executive director, gave me some useful background for his organization.

Jerry Hilecher, Steve Keeley and Dave Bledsoe were as gentlemanly to me as they are on court. Shannon Wright and Peggy Steding set examples for their sex that suggest the women's sports movement is not a transient phenomenon.

Charlie Brumfield is simply the most engaging professional athlete I have ever met. His own personal strengths and weaknesses sometimes parallel and sometimes contradict the strengths and weaknesses of pro sports. I enjoyed the inconsistency.

Contents

In 1969, if you had moved to San Diego and were a racquet-ball/paddleball enthusiast, you quickly would have looked up an organization identified as the PPA—Pacific Paddleball Association. There you would have met either Carl Loveday, Chuck Hanna, or myself, three active participants in the sport of racquetball. However, at that time I was just a neophyte sitting at the feet of two gurus of racquetball—that is, these men and other members of the PPA were somehow endowed with special knowledge and techniques associated with becoming a national racquetball champion, and I certainly had that objective in mind.

So that you do not discount this belief as merely a myth, a brief look at the record book shows that San Diegans have won five of eight national titles. Humbly, I must take credit for four of the national titles. Personally, I have won every national and international title available in racquetball today. For two years, I won twenty-seven pro events in a row. I cannot help but feel much of my success results from the early years spent with the gentlemen at the PPA.

My success and the mystique associated with the PPA credited the image that there was some secret to racquetball and it was only through migrating to San Diego and associating yourself with these people that you could become a national champion. The reason for that myth is really twofold. One, the PPA had an isolated court behind the house of a local doctor and all training and practice sessions were conducted in private. Therefore it would appear as if the most talented racquetball players would emerge from some isolated area and move through racquetball competition without ever having to extend themselves.

Steve Keeley, a Michiganite, had been looking for the secret to paddleball and, hopefully, racquetball, and was convinced it could only be found in San Diego. He quickly moved to this city and shortly thereafter emerged as one of the SPOH's top players. He was followed a year later by Steve Strandemo, a Minnesotan, whose promise in the sport was not visible until after his move to San Diego. The accomplishments of these players only added to the lore that San Diego was the place to go if one wanted to move into the top ranks of racquetball.

Today the top eight professional racquetball players in the world reside in San Diego. Almost all except myself migrated to this city between 1970 and 1976.

There are other reasons why San Diego was an ideal spot for the growth of racquetball. We generally enjoy good weather. Therefore the seasonal nature of the sport has no meaning, as it does in other parts of the country. Today a club owner in Chicago may find his facility empty in June or July when the weather changes. However, in San Diego we enjoy racquetball year-round, rarely noting any changes in season. Combine these two facts with one of the first official public racquetball clubs to come into existence in 1971, and you have the talent, climate, and facilities to breed champions.

It helps in understanding the migration to San Diego or the notion that San Diego is the mecca of racquetball if you think of the top players as members of a minority group. There certainly hasn't been any real money in the sport. Therefore its attraction must lie in areas best understood by the individual alone. His need to reinforce his own incentives and goals is dependent upon having an audience or a comrade to share these goals with. Movement to San Diego provided a source of satisfaction for these needs. Much of our time training was spent in after-game sessions discussing the pros and cons of our performance and ways we might improve.

The Singles Invitational in 1971 brought the sixteen top players of the game together, and tournaments became more than an opportunity to compare skill but also a gathering of Hobbits for the telling of tales and re-energizing of commitments. The sport quickly outgrew the fraternity atmosphere we found necessary and enjoyed in the early seventies, but among a handful of top professionals, these memories and the need to share them with others has created the impression of a "cult" difficult to join, because membership is characterized and aggrandized by time and experience. Having so many players and being so close to where many a championship has been held and champions born have created a fever among Southern Californians for racquetball that is quickly spreading and becoming a national phenomenon.

Evidence of this exists in the fact there are in excess of a hundred court clubs in the San Diego/Orange County area alone, with more coming into existence almost monthly. I can think of no champion in the sport today who has not spent some time in San Diego developing his skill and associating with the players in this area. Players like Roger Souders, Dave Charleson, Bob Martin, Bob McInerney, Chuck Hanna, Carl Loveday, Jim Trent, and John Halverson have very little national fame, but all played a major part in building the sport of racquetball in San Diego and influencing many national players.

Before you dismiss these ramblings as the exaggerated nostalgia of an aging professional, keep in mind that today's superstar (nineteen-year-old Marty Hogan), who has yet to win a national title, is now living in San Diego. They raise them in St. Louis, but we polish the pig iron in San Diego.

One of the happy jobs of an editor at any publishing house is attempting to pick trends before they happen—the hoola hoop, the miniskirt, the hustle—though obviously the happiest part of clairvoyance is being right. Lindy Hess, at Doubleday, has an active brain that doesn't only focus on life's larger issues. She has an eye for those apparently trivial pockets of activity and concluded that there was more to racquetball than a fleeting fad.

Without doing research on the motivation of why people play racquetball and thereby gaining insight on the sport's potential for expansion, Lindy determined that there was a fever in the West that was not dissimilar to the gold fever of a century ago. Bright dreams, adventure, physical struggle, and being wide open to everyone's participation were common themes to both phenomena. There is a likelihood that racquetball will become a cult far more comprehensive than golf in the 1960s and tennis ten years ago did.

Gene Scott was chosen as the author precisely because he does not play racquetball. It was felt that if racquetball had a legitimate claim as the most spectacular growth sport in the land, it would be more credible to hear this conclusion from an outsider rather than from one inside the game's frenetic core where prejudice and passion might flame opinion way past realistic appraisal.

Besides, Scott has been in the eye of the recent tennis hurricane and has seen firsthand and, on occasion, has influenced firsthand the wild growth of his sport. The parallel of racquetball to tennis is natural and lends a critical, comparative backdrop to where racquetball may be in a space-age future.

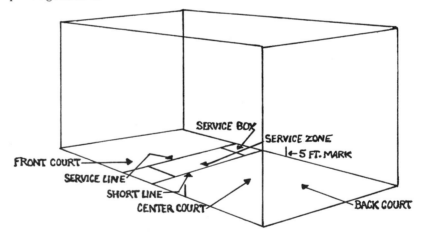

The Court

What is racquetball? The game has questionable origins, which will be explored later at length, but suffice to say at this juncture that racquetball is only eight years old and is played in an enormous stark white room —like squash—that measures twenty feet high by twenty feet wide by forty feet long. The rectangle is exactly the same size as a handball court. There are no windows in the room, though the trend is to have at least the backwall all glass, and fanatic futurists have already constructed courts with three walls (front, back, and one side) solid glass from the ceiling to the floor.

The sport is primarily a singles game, the object of which is to smack a bouncy rubber ball with a small racquet against the front wall until one player misses or drops in exhaustion.

A game consists of twenty-one points, and, unlike squash or tennis, you can only win points when serving. A match until recently was two out of three games, but in a major rules change, the sport's governing fathers decreed that an eleven- or fifteen-point sudden-death tiebreak would replace the final game when the match leveled at one game each.

The game starts with the server standing in the service zone, bouncing the ball, and hitting it at the front wall so that it lands beyond the back edge of the service zone (short line).

There seem to be more regulations governing the serve than any other part of the game. A half-dozen boobie traps await the novice's attempt simply to start the rally going. Normally the server gets two chances to put the ball in play, but if the ball doesn't hit the front wall first, it skips on the floor or strikes a sidewall first, the server loses his turn immediately. Losing the right to serve is called a "sideout." Yet, if the first serve hits the front wall and carries clear to the backwall without bouncing on the floor, it's a fault, but the server is entitled to a second serve.

If the server is hit by his own delivery, it results in a "sideout."

The receiver must stand at least five feet past the short line (server's box), and his choice of shots in returning the ball is virtually unlimited. He can hit one, two, or three walls—and even the ceiling—as long as the ball strikes the front wall before bouncing on the floor. Like tennis or squash, the rally lasts until a player misses or the ball bounces twice.

Who is playing racquetball? High real-estate costs have been blamed for the game's restricted growth in the East. Don't believe it. Developers have fought monstrous zoning wars in the law courts to win approval for constructing far bigger, more costly indoor tennis facilities than any racquetball installation. Indeed, eager entrepreneurs argue that comparative court costs ($70,000 per racquetball court and $150,000 per indoor tennis court) make racquetball a better investment than tennis.

No, there must be a darker reason why racquetball hasn't yet exploded in the Big Apple. It probably comes down to a theme that has repeatedly shattered the visions of countless dreammakers who come to New York with stars in their eyes and depart with dust in their pockets. New York City is culturally spoiled and saturated, and to change the habits or to catch the attention of its sated residents requires a Second Coming with the original cast. So for now, a sweaty no-tradition gym sport played with a plain bouncy ball does not grip the passion of blasé New Yorkers. This will change. And women players, who are a million strong, will force it. There are countless female athletes who are looking for exercise without frills. Tennis takes too long to learn and is too expensive indoors. Squash is also complicated for a beginner and discriminates against women by the very nature of the private men's club and school facilities where the game is played.

Racquetball, with no tradition and no aristocratic origin to overcome and without the intimidating clothes culture of tennis to surmount is easy to embrace. And while none of the three million racquetballers take their sport lightly, none take it too seriously either. It isn't easy to take a bouncy rubber ball seriously.

It's one thing to have an author explore the history and cult of racquetball as an objective reporter, but how can his ability as a teacher be authenticated? Simple.

Scott has played, written, and promoted tennis at the highest professional level for twenty years. Racquetball has only existed as a pro sport for five years, but teaching techniques and analytic ability fortunately have a comprehensive carry-over quality to all racquet sports.

Furthermore, Scott spent hours with both Charlie Brumfield and Steve Strandemo, two of the world's best players and the most articulate of the pros—to ferret out personal playing habits that could be integrated into a standard instruction code for everyone.

One intriguing fact the author quickly discovered is that even among racquetball experts there is disagreement concerning both method and terms. For example, three of the leading instruction books describe the famous Garfinkle serve differently. What one calls the Garfinkle, another calls the reverse Garfinkle. (The Garfinkle serve is a delivery that hits the front wall and then the left sidewall close to the seam and caroms crosscourt to your opponent's forehand. The reverse Garfinkle is its mirror image hitting the front wall, right sidewall, and landing deep in the backhand court.)

Also, there is no clearly articulated difference between the lob and the garbage serves, both being used as a change of pace, the principal difference being the degree of arc. But the distinction is a difficult one to master, especially if a beginner asks his instructor, "Is a low lob the same as a high garbage serve?"

This is not to disparage the current instruction volumes. Far from it. Teaching methods have been forced to move at a lightning pace primarily because the high-speed ball and glass court have altered the game radically from the control game of the past. Players and officials have both done a miraculous job adjusting.

What the inconsistency in teaching indicates is that there is a whole world of modern instruction technique that has yet to be explored. Racquetball is at the frontier of this world. It's an exciting prospect for both players and spectators to think that the incredible pace and action already inherent in racquetball will accelerate dramatically as new methods evolve.

One of the attractions of racquetball is that the equipment is cheap. It costs (and weighs) a ton to outfit a young hockey or football player, and golf and tennis have become so fashion-conscious that bare minimums are scoffed at in favor of carefully co-ordinated uniforms for every playday. Horrors to the unchic athlete who wears the same color combination twice in the same weekend.

However, in racquetball, attitudes toward clothes are totally reverse. Indeed, if a racquetballer arrived in all white or matching colored tennis shorts and top, he would look like a fag. Double-knit shorts and bright flowing polo shirts are simply too much clothes for racquetball.

This thinking makes sense in that if great emphasis is placed on speed of foot and hand, the Olympic-type track short and shirt are perfect models. They would be examples for tennis too if that sport were not snowed by the mentality of fashion houses that need high style and variation to turn a profit.

Colored gym shorts—the ones with the reverse V cut wide up both thighs—and T-shirts are *de rigueur* for racquetball. High-top basketball sneakers are worn by those who need ankle support; otherwise, everyone wears standard leather low cuts identical to those used in tennis. There is a trend to high socks—just below the knee—that is a half concession to style and half to cold courts.

Few players use sweatlets but most do wear some form of leather gloves for better gripping, and anyone with long hair wears a headband. Eyeguards should be mandatory—so great are the risks for injury from both ball and racquet—but they are ugly and suffer the same disdain that goalie masks and helmets did only a few years ago in professional hockey. Sooner or later the ego will give way to common sense, and already the St. Louis Jewish Community Center requires eyeguards for every competitor.

Wood racquetball racquets are virtually obsolete—tennis may never make this total transition—and are either aluminum or Fiberglas. Their shape is either owl's head or teardrop, the main difference being design, though the owl's-head face is smaller, with a smaller sweet spot but greater power when the ball makes contact smack in the center.

There is a myth among racquetball experts that Fiberglas provides greater control because the ball stays on the strings longer. This would be true if the racquet itself didn't move like a sling. But the whip effect of Fiberglas means greater power but less control, while aluminum frames are stiff, giving greater control. The properties of aluminum include being stiff, which causes greater vibration and tends to cause tennis elbow more quickly than Fiberglas. This disadvantage is partially offset by aluminum's greater durability. Eighty per cent of the top twenty pros use Fiberglas, which means that power is more important than control.

All racquetball racquets (which can measure no more than nine inches wide and eighteen long) are strung with nylon between twenty-five and thirty-two pounds, which is so loose that power is added through a trampoline action. The fact that no one uses gut strings is explained by the pros and manufacturers as a consequence of nylon producing more power and control at lower tensions, which is an impossible —though desirable—combination.

Listening to different equipment makers explain the playing characteristics of their product is intriguing because their analysis is eclectic rather than scientific. One has only to ask two leading executives from competitive firms whether a smaller racquet face can generate more power than a larger one because of its greater potential head speed—and get two totally different answers—to realize that manufacturing decisions are more emotional than rational. This response fits the racquetball experience itself, for which enthusiasm is beyond thoughtful attempts to explain or harness the sport's wild expansion.

For instance, none of the racquetball manufacturers in 1977 have sophisticated testing devices such as air tunnels, stress machines, X-ray devices, and hitting devices to research the properties of materials and products.

There is so much demand for racquets and balls that companies can scarcely keep up with production schedules. This partially explains why racquet people recommend nylon rather than gut and twenty-five to thirty-two pounds for stringing. Tighter stringing with gut would result in ten times the string breakage, which would mean very unhappy customers. Also, the current crop of racquets have irregular enough gromet and stringhole construction that they could not tolerate tight string jobs.

The fact is that the manufacturers haven't had time in the cyclonic racquetball boom to learn the dynamics of gut and nylon racquets at various tensions. Questions such as whether the ball leaves before the racquet has imparted its power, or whether Brumfield's racquet or his arm impart the power haven't been asked yet. But as the boom crescendos, new companies will enter the marketplace with streamlined technology and will produce better-performing equipment just to be able to compete properly. Graphite racquets, composites, and plastic foam materials haven't yet been developed, but with six million players predicted for 1980, new product lines will surface like bubbles from a champagne punch.

Why is it that historians—whether it be their account of the Peloponnesian or Napoleonic wars, the presidential election of 1948, or the Giants-Colts football playoff in 1958—*can't get the facts straight?* The answer is partially found in the old chestnut: If three reporters covered the same fire, the stories would be so different the reader would be suspicious that any of the newsmen saw the blaze at all.

It's true that events and how they happen may be subject to as many different interpretations as eyes that saw the event. Racquetball is no different. How, when, and where racquetball began is unclear. Apparently no one thought the game was important enough to record what was happening and when, which left its history to facile imagination rather than clear recollection.

There are three general phases in the history of racquetball. The first traces its origin back to the Kings of antiquity. When Louis IX played jeu de paume in 1245 in Vincennes, France, he was the royal forerunner to a closetful of court sports, including lawn tennis, hard racquets, squash, paddle tennis, platform tennis, racquets and racquetball. Handball, which in the 1960s was the hostile rival to racquetball, points its beginnings to the time of primitive man when two Neanderthals played catch with a rock. Bare hands gave way to leather thongs to ease the pain, and then plain wood paddles were substituted for the still faint of hand. New games were the result of local innovators either improving or compromising the equipment and court space available. For instance, long before there were rubber balls, gamesplayers had to improvise with whatever materials would bounce, however erratically. Cloth bindings, twine, and even human hair were some of the fibers once used to make a ball.

The lore of these ancient games is enthralling, and if we think that everyone takes their sport too seriously today, the matter is popped back into perspective with the reminder that in the early 1600s public tennis was banned in France because families were betting so heavily on exhibitions. This sort of mentality was not unique to the seventeenth century. In the 1950s, racquetball (then called both paddleball and paddle racquets) was banned from many community centers where over 95 per cent of all handball courts existed.

Major Clopton Wingfield, who is called the modern inventor of tennis, was responsible for a major change ultimately affecting racquetball, which was the introduction of a simple rubber ball replacing the all-cloth core of a thousand years before.

The second phase in the evolution of racquetball is more critical than the first. This was the time when the embryo was first recognizable as the infant from which all good things would spring.

In 1898, Frank Peer Beal founded paddle tennis in his family's backyard in Albion, Michigan. Later as Rev. Beal in Greenwich Village, New York, he was looking for an inexpensive outdoor recreation for his playground children and recalled his college-days invention, which halved the area of the tennis court, making the court thirty-nine feet by eighteen feet. He decreed that short-handled wooden paddles and a hard rubber ball be used instead of strung tennis racquets and felt-covered tennis balls. The game was simple to learn because the paddle made control easy, and the game was cheaper to play and required much less space than tennis.

In the early 1920s, tennis players above the American frost line were left without sport in wintertime—unless their family name was Whitney, Phipps, Mellon, Carnegie, or Cutting, in which case an indoor tennis palace was constructed with the same care and indulgence that created the manor house itself. But there were fewer than twenty-five indoor tennis courts in the country then—compared to ten thousand indoor facilities today—not exactly an exciting prospect for the year-round fanatic. As a result, tennis players resorted to the next best thing, playing in a handball or squash court for practice.

Squash tennis was one of the early creations in the East for the frustrated winter tennis player. On the other hand, paddleball was a hybrid game for the midwestern tennis player who sought refuge in the handball court until the snow melted. The full-length tennis racquet was found to be too unwieldy, and two solutions evolved. Wooden paddles (from paddle tennis) were substituted, or else the tennis bat was sawed off near the throat. The games played were almost identical except for the scoring, which depended on the background of the player. If the player was familiar with handball, a twenty-one-point game was used. If the prep-school culture prevailed, a fifteen-point—squash-scoring—game dominated. And there was enormous crossover—one player using a wood paddle, the other a cut-off strung implement—whatever was handy that afternoon. By and large, the evolution narrowed to playing a fifteen-point game when it was played in a squash court and a twenty-one-point game when a hand-ball facility was trespassed.

The variation of the ball used was multiple. It really boiled down to a matter of which type ball—tennis, rover's fetch ball, or a child's rubber bouncer—you happened to have in your pocket.

Adding to the confusing smorgasbord of paddle-racquet sports was the invention in 1928 of platform tennis in Scarsdale, New York, by Fessenden S. Blanchard and James Cogswell. The importance of early platform tennis to racquetball was not its platform nor the surrounding wire screen nor its mininet, but the fact that the sport used paddle tennis racquets.

In a world of infinite variety and no rules, Earl Riskey is the man first credited in the late 1920s with attempting to standardize the game of paddleball, which was to become racquetball. Riskey became involved with the athletic department of the University of Michigan and adapted the basic handball rules for his sport. He elected to use the wooden paddle, and after rejecting both the tennis ball and a sponge rubber ball as too heavy, he devised a method of removing the wool nap from a tennis ball by soaking it in gasoline to get down to the black core.

Paddleball was boosted in the late 1930s by Harvey Bauss, who enabled the game to be selected as unofficial conditioner for the armed forces. The ball was made respectable in 1950 when Pennsylvania Tire and Rubber (now The General Tire & Rubber Co.) produced the "pinkie" to replace the ugly black bandit of Riskey's era.

In 1961, the first national paddleball tournament was staged and has continued as a regular—if anachronistic—event to this day. Paddleball has all but been swallowed by its more elegant brother racquetball, a fact that the four-time national paddleball champion, Steve Keeley, admits without remorse, one assumes, because Keeley was versatile enough to make the switch from ranking paddleballer to star racquetballer without much fuss. In fact, the switch was not that difficult and involved primarily the swapping of a gut-string racquet for an all-wood paddle. The scoring and court dimensions were virtually the same.

All this time, there was not a regular progression of paddleball to racquetball. Rather, it heaved and weaved mightily in every direction at once without organization, rules, or recognizable standards.

The man heralded as the father of racquetball, Joe Sobek, was the first to get his sport to use a strung racquet in 1949. Obviously this was not an innovation, because squash tennis had much earlier used a stubby tennis racquet, but he developed the theme to the extent that a new wood racquet was specifically designed for racquetball. And Sobek ferreted out a company that would develop a ball to specifications that he thought best for the game. But Sobek didn't consider that with all his changes, the game wasn't truly paddleball at all because it was no longer played with a paddle. He called his invention paddle rackets.

In 1968, the first national paddle rackets tournament was held in Milwaukee, and it provided a focus for all handball and paddleball players who slowly were beginning to switch over to Sobek's passion. Many of today's top racquetball players were outstanding paddleball stars, such as Charlie Brumfield, Bill Schmidke, Bud Muehleisen, Steve Keeley, Craig Finger, Paul Lawrence, and Bill Schultz. San Diego was the home of most of these top paddleballers and, as a result, began its reputation as the nerve center for all racquetball. The reputation was largely cosmetic in the beginning, and only recently has it fulfilled its own prediction as the core city of racquetball fanaticism.

The chief cultural force behind the expansion of racquetball was the Jewish Community Center. The St. Louis Junior Program, for example, has produced four of the top eight pros on tour. The JCC integrates a faith and lifestyle in all community programs. The entire family participates in the activity, and its strength is as solid as Little League baseball or Pop Warner football. The Jewish centers have become the farm teams and breeding grounds for future racquetball superstars.

In 1969 paddle rackets was renamed "racquetball" by either Bud McInerney, a San Diego tennis pro, or Bob Kendler, a wealthy Chicago real-estate builder and the father of handball, depending on whose attic you're searching for court sports history.

Racquetball was still in utter disarray as an organized sport until its first national championships that same year in St. Louis when Kendler, with a keenly developed entrepreneurial nose, was asked to inject his wisdom as the douanier of handball to a new sport that was daring like a pinwheel in colorful chaos.

Kendler promptly established the International Racquetball Association at the 1969 nationals, but quickly switched field when he saw the

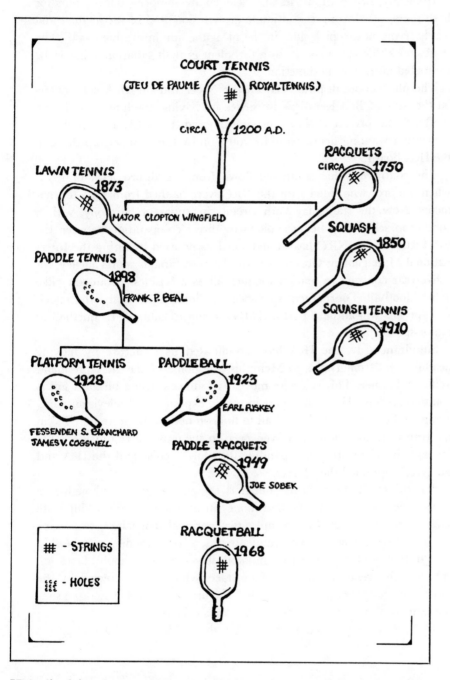

IRA dissolving into a mighty bureaucratic fumble needing the entire twelve-man-board's approval to make the most mundane of decisions. Kendler moved his marbles and his energy to found a brand-new organization, the National Racquetball Club. The purpose of the NRC was devoted to the development of professional racquetball, and toward that end it established the first pro tour in 1973 with a total purse of $50,000 in six cities. Today that prize money has more than doubled to $120,000 for twelve cities, and even the original IRA has strengthened its organization under the leadership of President Bill Tanner and Executive Director Tom McKie. The IRA scheduled a five-city pro tour in 1976 offering $8,000 in each—identical to the NRC money.

Ironically, Leach Industries and Seamco are the principal sponsors for both tours, recognizing the ultimate growth potential of racquetball and wisely trying not to pick sides in the picayune administrative hassle. The feud shows that some energy in a turbulent growth situation is apt to be dissipated in the wrong direction.

The philosophic dispute between the NRC and the IRA still centers on the issue of Bob Kendler's insistence on having absolute control over the NRC, his private business corporation, and the NRA, a nonprofit organization wanting decisions to be voted on by the membership through the IRA board.

The controversy has simmered down from an absurd level in 1974, when the pros who sided with the NRC were banned from IRA tournaments. Now the stars play both circuits in apparent harmony, with a conflict in scheduling being avoided by direct co-operation between the two factions. The NRC has strengthened its position by hiring the International Management Group, the world's most famous sports agency, for a five-year contract to market racquetball as a business commodity like golf or football. Tournament sponsorship, clinics, exhibitions, and television specials will all be a part of IMG's vision to catapult racquetball to major-sports status.

Simultaneously, the IRA has consolidated its structure by moving headquarters from Dallas to Memphis, the home of the IRA president, William Tanner. This is a wise move, as Tanner's strong business suit is communications. He is an expert in media exposure and television packaging, and one expects racquetball to flourish both in print and on TV in the future. It is obvious, however, even to the most naïve outsider, that an explosive chemistry for expanding the sport is possible if the IRA and the NRC combined their forces.

Surprisingly, the schism has not hurt the game's growth, though it is easy to see the waste of time and money in having two groups duplicate each other's purpose—for example, two national magazines, two tours, two executive directors, two presidents. Each has a modest membership of ten thousand out of three million players. Both should focus on enrolling the gigantic number of outsiders who are all affected by the force of each association but don't feel the urgency to join when the simple benefits of playing—not debating—are so obvious.

The first era of racquetball is over. But the end is just the beginning.

So what's the fuss about racquetball? In 1967 there was no such sport. By the next year, two remote racquet games were picked clean of their best ingredients and a brand-new one—racquetball—emerged. In 1968, there were two hundred thousand players. In 1976 were three million, and by 1980 the projected figure is ten million. If statistics in abstraction deaden your understanding, a simple comparison is helpful. Platform tennis (affectionately known as paddle tennis), which presently enjoys a rage of some sorts because of a new professional tour, has but four hundred thousand players. Squash, which has two hundred years of history behind it and has also been fueled by regular pro tournaments, lists only five hundred thousand participants. Racquetball in eight years has three million players.

The current craze over racquetball makes the tennis boom of the early 1970s look like glacier movement by comparison. There are already more racquetball players than there were tennis players in 1960. And tennis had then been played for almost ninety years. Just as tennis had a moment that triggered its popular explosion, waking it from a century-long sleep, racquetball also had that threshold point when it went berserk. The difference was that racquetball's fiery launching happened simultaneously with its birth.

Tennis, on the other hand, was suffocated by its birth—a product of an idle British military man, Major Clopton Wingfield, assembling components of various other games (racquets, royal tennis) and presenting his amalgam as a relaxing diversion for English garden parties. The rich quickly adopted the sport as a birthright of sorts and never let it out of their sight or country clubs for a moment. What a deadly beginning to overcome!!

Tennis dragged along chained to the aristocracy—the rules of tennis would not permit an amateur to taint himself by competing against a professional until 1968—until finally enough fresh ideas blew into the sport to smash it open and away from the governing fathers who had held it captive for almost a century.

Following the course of tennis is a useful diversion to help understand the pervasive fever of racquetball. All of the modern court sports owe their historic allegiance to tennis, which itself traces its origins through the Persian invasion of France, the French monasteries and Gallic rulers, and finally the popularization of royal tennis so adored by Henry VIII, who played with gusto at Hampton Court. Then Wingfield collected a bunch of racquet pastimes played only by a handful and named his concoction spairistike—a title that gives us an idea of the clipped mentality of those playing it. Lawn tennis surfaced from "sticky"—as it was so cutely nicknamed by the cutesies playing—and tennis as we know it today was on its way, though hardly at a roller coaster's pace.

The grandest irony of all is that tennis, with its proud tradition, would have continued a progression in darkness had not five or six events occurred successively. Open tennis, television, Chris Evert's Cinderella debut at Forest Hills, Billie Jean King vs. Bobby Riggs, the indoor tennis boom, the metal racquet craze, and Jimmy Connors vs. Rod Laver all contributed to expanding the game past its stuffy and stifling background. The sport had the requisite ingredients to be super popular—the equipment was inexpensive, it provided quick exercise, and it was recreation for a lifetime, unlike football, baseball, or other team sports whose "playing" culture ceased after college.

How did racquetball ascend so explosively without the hallowed traditions of tennis? Simple. Racquetball boomed *because* of an absence of tradition, not in spite of it.

Tradition is a holy word for civilization's politics and culture. Why? Because customs that are honored for centuries give citizens a sense of order. The unknown and the unpredictable have been shibboleths to all societies on the premise that brand-new ideas can eat you up. Literally eat you up. If foreigners came to your village in Persian, Roman, or Revolutionary War times, there was a fear that the invaders would kill your children, rape your wife, and possibly eat *you* up.

For society as a whole, tradition was probably a good idea for a while —maybe until the end of the eighteenth century—but modern sociologists, psychologists, and even biofeedbackers are desperately trying to get us to strip away some of our environmental hangups, so we can proceed more hastily to a more advanced socioculture. What's this got to do with the racquetball cult? Plenty. Racquetballers had no background cultures or countercultures to overcome. There were no gentle myths to destroy such as all-white clothes, don't show your emotions, stiff upper lip, and a sacred ready position, and keep the ladies and kids out of my club, or at least off my court. Alvin Toffler was not thinking of racquetball in 1970 when he wrote the famous behavorial book *Future Shock*, but he could have been. Toffler explained that all society is modifying their behavior patterns at a superaccelerated rate of change. Modern technological and media advancement can now alter in two years community standards that once might have taken a decade to develop.

Racquetball symbolized change itself and was, therefore, unafraid of change. On the other hand, the deadened imaginative powers of the general sporting-goods manufacturers was appalling. For example, tennis racquets were made of wood until 1967, even though there were no regulations about size, weight, or material. In that year the Wilson Sporting Goods Co., borrowing René La Coste's tubular steel design, halfheartedly marketed the T2000 frame. In spite of Wilson's sleepy salesmanship, the racquet took off because three players using the T2000 dominated Forest Hills that same year. Suddenly metal racquets of all shapes and designs glutted the marketplace. A further illustration of the almost paranoid resistance to change was the fact that all tennis balls were white until 1970, when a simple experiment with yellow at the suggestion of a television director resulted in 75 per cent of all tennis balls now being *nonwhite*.

Racquetball had no such murky mentality to overcome. The pioneers of the game—it's a laugh to think of 1968 as pioneer days, but that's what knocking tradition will do for you (tomorrow is a new wilderness) —simply looked around and saw that the black color of a handball and paddle tennis ball was not visible. Now, yellow, green, red, and blue racquetballs are on the market, and the manufacturers—Vittert, Leach, and Seamco—work with the pioneers of the sport to search for better ideas. My God! A sports-company executive following the directive of those who play and run the game? You won't find such heresy in other sports, but then again you won't find such meteoric growth and popularity in other sports.

Racquetball is essentially the people's squash, with no snob hangups, no club membership committees to penetrate, and no archaic association to overcome in order to change a rule here or a custom there that might benefit the game. If you think I'm exaggerating the debilitating effect that society and tradition might have on sport, let me offer one devastating example. Of the five hundred thousand squash players in this country, the lady players proudly point out that there are almost twenty thousand ladies playing squash. Their pride probably puffs the real number participating by as much as 40 per cent, but inflated figures aside, what a dismal statistic to use your paradigm for popularity. Gangway. There are almost a million *women* racquetballers.

Racquetball is played at YMCAs, YWCAs, civic centers, hotels, resorts, and commercial clubs where woman are welcomed with the glee usually reserved for a stock dividend.

One of the prime reasons for the instant success of racquetball is that it can be learned in an instant. If you can count to twenty-one and hit a barn door with a rock, you can play racquetball immediately. It's a very easy game to learn and enjoy quickly. This, of course, is not true of tennis, where it takes almost two years to master the rally. Most of the learning process in tennis is spent fetching the ball as it hits the fence, the bottom of the net, or the neighbor's lawn, which is also excellent exercise but scarcely what was contemplated when you started. Yet in beginner's racquetball the ball always comes back to you like a heat-seeking missile. You don't spend any of the learning process playing fetch.

Even in squash, a premium is placed on stroking technique and all-around racquet ability, while racquetball, with a bigger, bouncier ball and larger racquet face, require only rudimentary skills at the beginner and intermediate level.

Another advantage racquetball has over the older traditional games, particularly squash, is that since racquetball is new, there are not a multitude of old court facilities that perpetuate the anachronisms of the past. For instance, squash courts are totally enclosed white closets, the vast majority of which have no spectator facility. And in even those that do have a viewing gallery, the space can only accommodate 150 people maximum, hardly a number to enthuse the masses. Recently there has been a progressive move in squash to build a glass backwall as a standard fixture. But what about all those traditional facilities in existence? The cost of tearing down the back wall and replacing it with glass is prohibitive, so until squash grows with more than ministeps, most of the game will be played on courts where the action will be a virtual secret to spectators.

Because racquetball was born in 1968, 95 per cent of the courts built since then have at least one glass wall. The phenomenon of the glass wall is not only a bonanza to the spectator's expansion of the sport, it is also a direct catalyst for participation growth as well. Acting on the same theory that no one would ever go to a discotheque unless they could be seen dancing or look at others dancing, visibility in a racquetball court encourages the players and the viewers to play even more. Think about it. No one would think of going to a disco—no matter how zippy the music—unless it was packed with people. Traditionalists would have us believe that if you truly enjoyed your sport, you would never need anybody watching. The tradition-gagged have not talked to behaviorists who point out that even babies must have the noises and voices of people around to develop properly.

There are two men who are pioneers in racquetball who sacrificed a core part of their life to develop a game when rewards were nonexistent. There are others who were a critical part of racquetball's history or its present. But Bob Kendler and Charlie Brumfield are singled out from the rest because they personify the flaming intensity that stokes the game's prodigious growth.

Kendler and Brumfield are also chosen because they represent two totally different segments of racquetball's cult. Kendler is the seventy-one-year-old wizard administrator who picked up racquetball when it was a disorganized pile of cards. Brumfield, twenty-eight, is a scholar who gave up a career in the law to become the consummate professional. It is as if this pair accepted their destiny as the game's master craftsmen, setting an unparallelled standard of excellence for their successors to shoot for.

Others contributed important segments that had impact on the game's ultimate development—old timers like Sobek, Riskey, and Bauss and modern men like William Tanner, the IRA president, and Leach Industries vice president Charles Drake. But no one will ever make the wholesale innovative injections that Kendler did to the sport's superstructure and that Brumfield did to the sport's techniques and tournament record books. It can't be done again. The pair covered too much of racquetball's history and future in the same swath.

Bob Kendler injects passion into anything he does. He had the proper background to assemble the helter-skelter parts of two offshoot racquet sports and preside over their coalition. Twenty-five years earlier Kendler had challenged the AAU, which he felt was stifling the development of handball. Kendler, a winner of five national doubles titles himself, formed the U. S. Handball Association and ran his own national tournament, a move that caused the AAU to bar him and later sue him for a million dollars. Avery Brundage, the intimidating official who ran the Olympics like a dictator, was called in to arbitrate the matter, and decided that it was not relevant who had the "right" to run handball but who was best for the sport. Kendler won that decision in a cakewalk—not too many have taken on the AAU and won—and proceeded to standardize courts, equipment, and the rules, and essentially returned the game to the players.

At the nadir of "racquetball's" chaos during the 1968 National Paddle Racquets Championship in Milwaukee, Kendler was asked to unify paddle racquets and paddleball players and lead them out of the darkness.

Bob Kendler.

He agreed so long as he could have absolute authority to "take over" and implement changes wherever he felt needed. It wasn't a great deal to ask because there wasn't to much to take over on the 1968 racquetball scene.

The key ingredient that Kendler provided initially was making contact with the major Jewish Community Centers and YMCAs around the country—particularly in St. Louis and Houston. These centers were dominated by handball players hostile to the racquetballers taking up court time. But because Kendler had been the major force in handball for twenty-five years, he was given a sympathetic ear to getting racquetball started in the YMCAs and JCCs. Kendler persuaded his handball friends in St. Louis to let the local JCC be the site for the first national racquetball tournament, in 1969. The YMCAs and the JCCs were the single biggest factor in the growth of racquetball and development of players around the country, and Kendler was the man who co-ordinated the communication among those organizations and racquetballers.

The court club phenomenon certainly did not contribute to the early growth of racquetball. It took advantage of the beginning boom. There simply were not enough court clubs in 1969 to act as a catalyst for the sport's start-up progress. Kendler was the catalyst.

Kendler helped found the International Racquetball Association at the first national championship in St. Louis. In addressing this fledging organization, Kendler emphasized that he wanted to keep the game simple, which meant standardizing its rules, and to keep its costs down, bringing racquetball within reach of millions of part-time athletes. At this meeting, he decreed that the name of the sport would forever be racquetball, and though others are given credit for thinking of the name, Kendler was the man with enough executive hammer to make the name stick.

Kendler also ensured that court dimensions would be uniform. "Did you know that paddleball was sometimes played in squash courts? You should have seen the scars on the faces of some of those players. I was just trying to keep someone from being killed," he explained. (He considered the danger factor so compelling that he totally discouraged doubles and persuaded manufacturers to install a racquet guard around the top.)

Kendler soon convinced Seamco to design and manufacture an official IRA ball that would throw off royalties to the Association and provide a standardized price of equipment. Seamco was at first hesitant to market a ball for a sport that in the past had more splinter groups than a beach boardwalk. "That's all changed," Kendler insisted, and he backed up his conviction with his personal guarantee to purchase the difference if Seamco didn't sell 240,000 balls in two years. (Kendler wasn't ever close to having to go into his own pocket on this venture.)

Bob Kendler's energy continued on every front as he encouraged use of a colored ball for greater visibility in glass courts, where the black ball was difficult to see. The green Seamco was also better for television, which has always been in Kendler's mind for the ultimate breakaway of racquetball. He also listened to the players and agreed that a more lively ball would allow full use of all four walls plus the ceiling ball. He was even the forerunner for glass-walled courts, as he "invented" the glass back wall for handball in 1943.

Perhaps his greatest achievement in racquetball was his settling of the raucous "range war" between handball players and racquetballers that had been brewing since the early 1950s when paddleballers and paddle racquet players began invading handball courts. Naturally, as interest in "racquetball" accelerated, the "range war" boiled accordingly. At the height of animosity between the two groups, Kendler, president of the U. S. Handball Association, took over as leader of the rival International Racquetball Association. It was Kissinger diplomacy at a time Kissinger was applying for his first passport.

Kendler accomplished peace on three fronts. First, handball players were only using the nation's fifty thousand handball courts in YMCAs and YWCAs for five hours a day during lunch hours and the afternoon and early evening. Racquetball people would play at any time of the day over a sixteen-hour period. Women and children occupied the courts in the morning and afternoon when businessmen could not play, and court operators soon learned that by proper scheduling, dead time suddenly had become profitable.

In addition, there were many court clubs that were constructed after 1970 that took the pressure off the handball facilities, particularly in San Diego, where in 1968 an estimated ten thousand racquetballers were competing for space on a hundred courts. Kendler's best argument for the equal coexistence of the two hostile groups was that racquetball extended the playing life of a handball player by ten years. Handball is essentially a young man's game, and the switch to racquetball was convenient—the court was the same—and provided an option to athletes for whom the agonizing ache of hands and legs was no longer tolerable.

Kendler moved with such force and with such a broad reach that he affected everyone in the sport. He was bound to bruise feelings. The backlash to Kendler's role as racquetball's benevolent dictator came in the form of a strengthened IRA board of directors who challenged his unilateral fashion of decision-making. Where Kendler had previously been able to instantly correct any inefficiency on his own, changes now had to be approved by the twelve-member IRA board.

Kendler bridled at this intrusion on his original mandate to do things his own way, and, at the April 1973 International Tournament in St. Louis, he resigned as president. He immediately formed a rival organization, the National Racquetball Clubs, for the purpose of sponsoring a professional tour, and established the U. S. Racquetball Association as an all-amateur organization. Moving with customary alacrity, Kendler underwrote the first six pro tournaments himself in the fall of 1973.

Though the IRA jumped in to schedule a separate professional circuit in 1974, Kendler's tour is the most powerful in the land, and he endures as the game's commanding figure. And he continues to improvise. *National Racquetball* is the official magazine for the NRC and the USRA, and is easily the dominant publication in racquetball.

The crucial contribution Kendler made to racquetball was not in tangible improvements but in the emphasis he put on who should be playing the sport. Where handball actively discouraged women and children from playing, Kendler pursued the family relentlessly as representing the future of racquetball.

The slow-motion growth of squash and tennis until the 1970s was, in part, caused by a lack of interest in women's and children's participation. The U. S. Lawn Tennis Association did encourage junior tournament players, but not "just for the fun of it" players.

Women pros in tennis had to fight like desperados to win a semblance of dignity on tour, and it wasn't through efforts of officialdom that won them prize-money parity; it was one woman, Gladys Heldman, who pressured Philip Morris through one of its brands, Virginia Slims, to promote a separate series of ladies' professional tournaments.

Bob Kendler had to do the same thing for the professional women racquetballers by taking some sponsors' money away from the men's tour and putting it into the women's schedule. The protesting cries from the men pros who saw their modest purses being diluted further sounded like the beleagued wail of handballers who complained of racquetballers taking over their courts.

Kendler foresaw the contribution women could make in terms of utilizing dead afternoon and morning court times and as a positive market to encourage court club construction. The same argument held true for young people. In addition, Kendler pointed out that racquetball's greatest assets were the "sophisticated athletic clubs, the exclusive golf clubs, and the expensive tennis clubs, which rule out the family of modest means."

The facts that one million women and almost half a million youngsters under nineteen play racquetball justify Kendler's crusade.

Bob Kendler's eight-year association with racquetball is not a garden-variety flirtation—it is a steamy love affair. And when you interview Kendler with an eye to uncovering racquetball's history, you realize he doesn't talk about the grand old days or of the game's ancient lore, he talks about himself. This is the history of racquetball. His personal example provides a sound argument against decision by committee and that tradition may stifle—not encourage—new ideas and growth. But more, that one good man, energetic and with vision, can trigger a movement that while not possessing the impact of a religious crusade, has similar fanatic ingredients, and to those playing racquetball, is of identical cultural magnitude.

Charlie Brumfield, the self-proclaimed superstar of his sport, is the highest-paid man in racquetball, but his income doesn't approach the giants of basketball, football, hockey, or baseball. Charlie's 1976 total of seventy-five thousand was not earned with ease. He had to hustle in tournaments, endorsements, clinics, and personal appearances.

His hustle is just one sign of the man's passion. He is at the epicenter of racquetball's fanaticism. He has won more money and titles—including three national championships—than any three rivals combined. Brumfield has not just set records that will serve as a permanent example for future champions. His marks will be broken, but he will be remembered because he was the game's first superhero.

Brumfield, like Bob Kendler, is not admired in all circles. Brumfield whirls his arms and his voice around on court and off court, and his constant state of motion agitates many around him. But even his detractors

Charlie Brumfield.

admit that his effect of the game's strokes and strategy has been unrivaled.

Paradoxically, Brumfield's physique parallels racquetball's character. He is not a graceful athlete. Racquetball is not a graceful game. It is violent and aggressive. Their styles are in perfect sync.

Brumfield is the perfect specimen for racquetball's first hero. When he set a record in 1976 by winning seven out of ten tournaments, including the national title—a streak that will be difficult to duplicate—he did it without elegance. He does not cut a dashing figure on court. His socks droop lazily over thick ankles, his gym shorts fold on top of thick thighs with all the style of a sheet tossed over a cadaver. His appearance seems to shout, "Listen, boys, you don't have to have style to win at this game." The message is also important to comprehending the fanaticism intrinsic to racquetball. "Everyone can play. You don't have to be a superjock to get along in racquetball."

Brumfield followed his own message. After graduating with honors from San Diego State and completing law school there, he plunged himself into racquetball with ferocious dedication. He practiced seven hours a day, and when he wasn't playing racquetball he was playing badminton to improve his overhead for racquetball, and when it wasn't badminton, it was swimming to build up his stamina for racquetball.

The whole time he was a serious student of the sport. During practice sessions with Steve Keeley in the summer of 1971 he conceived of the ceiling ball, which is now a regular part of the defensive arsenal of every pro. He developed the best ceiling ball by going into the court alone and slapping high balls five hundred times until he was near exhaustion—or until the ball would regularly drop parallel to the back wall, whichever came first. That same summer, Brumfield, with Keeley's help, also invented the "Z" ball and the Around-the-Wall Ball. Both are defensive maneuvers to remove your opponent from the strategic center court position. The "Z" hits the front wall high, caroms off the left or right sidewall, and lands close to the back wall with little to shoot for. The ATW's purpose is the same, though it strikes a high sidewall first, then the front wall, and finally the opposite sidewall before bouncing deep in the backcourt. Though easier to execute than the "Z," it is not as effective, as the third-wall carom slows the ball down and makes it easier to anticipate.

To invent a new shot—one that may have been imagined but never seriously considered tactically—not only takes insight but also an astuteness that can visualize whether constant hours of practice will produce a shot that works.

Brumfield's technique of practicing by doing multiple repetitions of a single shot had been thought of before, but his single-mindedness in approach to solo sessions (where he would spend forty-five minutes hitting one stroke from a single area of the court) added a new dimension to learning—one that is emulated by virtually every child prodigy today.

Brumfield also introduced "psych" into racquetball to a degree that had never before been contemplated. His asking for a towel to wipe up a phantom sweat spot to destroy an opponent's momentum is legendary. His stalling tactics to get a rest or dissolve a foe's concentration have bordered on a rules infraction. And his intimidating catcalls after a winning rally have driven fear into his iciest competitors.

To win his twenty major championships, Brumfield was not only a pioneer but also an innovator. He had to be. The rules and equipment have changed rapidly in the past eight years, and while he is philosophic about the transitions, he has not always been happy about them. "I think glass walls impede the perfect play of racquetball. Sidewall and back-wall glass may be a necessary sacrifice for spectators, but front-wall glass is going too far.

"I don't care that it favors hard hitters; the gallery just won't experience racquetball at its best with wrap-around glass. How can you hit the ball when you can't see it?"

Brumfield sees glass affecting the entire game unless a manufacturer develops a two-way glass that does not hinder vision. Until that time, the faster ball and the all-glass court will mean shorter rallies.

"After a few shots, the ball is momentarily lost in a spectator's shirt, resulting in a mishit or complete miss. Control will disappear as a factor.

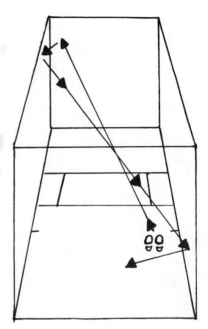

Flight of forehand Z Ball

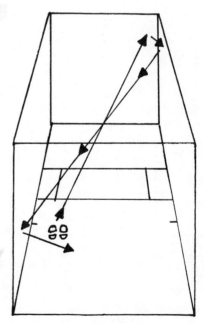

Flight of backhand Z Ball

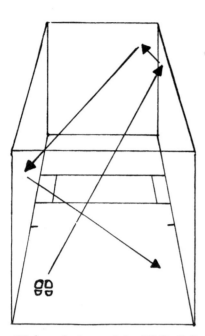

Flight of Around-the-Wall Ball
from backhand side

The ace serve will dominate because the second serve is so simple to put into play. It's unfortunate that the hustle and guts of the older champion may become obsolete."

Even if Brumfield's inputs to racquetball in terms of stroking theory, practice, and his playing records were not factors, his contribution to the sport's language world remain forever. The "Z" ball (a defensive shot that hits high front wall, sidewall, and backcourt), the "Around-the-Wall-Ball" (another defensive shot hitting high sidewall, front wall, opposite sidewall, and dropping into backcourt), the "reverse pinch," (a kill shot—front wall, sidewall), and "paralysis via analysis" (to choke) are all the products of Brum's fertile articulation. "Multifaceted attack," "coverage patterns," and "kill shot zones" are other examples of his phraseology for strategy.

Brumfield's mouth is not only imaginative and amusing but sometimes abrasive, such as when he concludes, "My ability to communicate will make me more money than the other pros will ever see. For example, Marty Hogan's the kind of guy that if he didn't know how to serve and shoot, he'd be out selling tacos."

At the same time he needles others, Brumfield does have a self-deprecative sense of humor that buffs the rough edges of his cockiness. He smiles as he talks of one day being picked for an American Express card ad that would have the caption, "You may not recognize me—or my sport." And then he explains why he has an unlisted telephone number in the San Diego directory: "Simply to cut down the hate calls."

Charlie Brumfield does have a sense of where he belongs in the order of racquetball's history. But Charlie won't let anyone speak for him. He has to say it himself.

"I think I'm going to be remembered like Ty Cobb is—the guy who came in with his spikes high. Not everybody liked him, but he sure was a helluva player."

Racquetball instruction books are first folios of sorts because the teaching techniques are as new as the sport itself. There is no fifty-year curve of learning devices, graphs, and illustrations. Instruction is at the beginning of its evolution, and over the next twenty years new concepts will emerge constantly. The theories will change not only because of improved techniques but because the equipment—principally the racquet, the ball, and the front glass wall—will be severely modified.

For example, the old heavy or dead ball forced the pro to be a control player. The risk of winging a ball an inch above the front-wall floor was too great if your opponent could get to it. The resulting retrieve meant the risk-taker had to tempt the odds again, going for that narrow kill zone close to the floor. Like the crapshooter who fires a few sevens and keeps his money on the "line," sooner or later the odds will catch up and he'll crap out—or in racquetball "sideout," by skipping the ball on the floor. The dice analogy is brought into focus if you realize that retrieving a kill attempt is the same as rolling a seven but not winning any money in the process.

With a fast ball, it's worth the risk to shoot for the kill. If you make it, there's no retrieve. You only have to roll one seven to collect your money. Next to the fast ball, the most controversial innovation in modern racquetball is the front-wall glass court. Both reduce vision and alter the game's nature drastically. With hand/eye speed impaired, rallies shorten to one- or two-stroke shootouts, and the importance of control and endurance is negated entirely. Already the all-glass court is being planned to accommodate television and spectators. A black or colored ball is easily seen against a white background, but when the backdrop is a mixture of black, shiny, and whatever color the fan in the first row is wearing, visibility is distorted altogether.

The loss of perception encourages the player to be a shooter. When a ball travels fast against a white wall, it's difficult enough to react to a near ace or near nick. But if the ball is fast and camouflaged—even momentarily—by the glass wall, it's almost impossible to retrieve.

The ceiling ball, so effective with a slower ball—not to be confused with the dead ball of the 1969 era—has lost its premier place in defensive arsenals because it now tends to carry the back wall and pop off in perfect position for a kill.

As a consequence of shorter rallies, the new game is criticized by top pros and spectators as contradictory to racquetball's original thesis of being easy to learn. With so much emphasis on power and speed, the stars don't feel they are being beaten in the sense that a strategically placed ball has outwitted them or forced a mishit, but rather that the ball travels so fast, they may never catch up to it.

To use an absurd example, it would be as if the front wall were solid black slate and the ball were a small black marble. Even if gently struck, it would ricochet around the court like a bumblebee gone berserk.

In spite of protestation above that there is no single way to grip a racquet, the grip must be the first lesson. Otherwise you might hold the racquet like a javelin, or worse, like a piece of toast.

Charlie Brumfield's trigger finger extension for the eastern forehand grip.

The "shake hands" grip is the most effective focal point. To find this grip, you simply lay the flat of your hand over the face of the strings and slowly bring your hand down toward the butt end and shake hands with the leather handle. The fingers should be slightly spread to avoid the clenched-fist grip, which restricts racquet feel. Control comes from the fingers, not the palm, which would dominate the stroke if the fingers were bunched together as if you were clutching a hammer. And no one has ever accused the swing of a hammer of being artful. Charlie Brumfield favors a trigger finger extension for even further control.

You can check to see if the hand is in the proper position by looking for a V formed along the side of the handle between your thumb and first or trigger finger. Whether you "choke up" on the handle or let the butt end lay in the fleshy part of your palm is a matter of personal preference. Experiment. Try both ways and halfway in between to see which feels more comfortable. "Choking up" accomplishes more control, while lowering your hand slightly off the racquet produces more power, resulting from the head being whipped faster by the wrist.

A controversy that has not yet raged to its full force simmers over whether you should change grips from the forehand to the backhand. The most commonly accepted theory is that you *should* change by rotating the racquet one-eighth turn clockwise (turning the hand counterclockwise accomplishes the same purpose). This practice surely will not continue. As the new crop of young professionals develops with fast balls and the glass court, a constant grip will become the rule. There isn't enough time to switch.

The older pros—Brumfield, Keeley, Schmidke, and Strandemo—surfaced at a time when the ball was slow and the control game dominated. Changing grips does aid in control, but not when you don't have a split second to make the adjustment. Already the sport's fastest hitter, nineteen-year-old Marty Hogan, leads the way with a single grip off both sides.

There is less controversy over the ideal angle for the racquet face in the hitting area. The top pros teach that the racquet should be absolutely up and down, square to the floor at the instant of contact. Stop-action photographs show that in reality the face top is tilted slightly backward over 50 per cent of the time at the moment of impact, the effect of which is to impart slight backspin on the ball. However, the instruction to keep the racquet free of incline at the hit point is sound, as it emphasizes that the bread-and-butter ground strokes—the kill and the pass—should be hit flat. The reason for this is that a racquetball ball compresses easily, and spins are neutralized the moment it hits the front wall at high speed —not like tennis or squash, where the ball is harder, making spin a critical component of every drive.

Since the above applies to both forehand and backhand, it is a natural transition to begin our discussion of the swing at this point.

The first part of the swing is the "setup," which is the equivalent of the ready position in tennis but that comes at a later stage in the stroke. With an opponent over seventy-eight feet away in tennis there is great emphasis on mechanically getting your racquet back before the ball is close to you. This is to give an easy rhythm to your game—one that will never leave you unprepared. As soon as the ball is stroked, you are supposed to bring the racquet back immediately into the ready position directly in front of your body. This discipline will prevent hurried jerky motions during a rally, which—in women's tennis, particularly—may pass over the net sixty times.

In racquetball there is no time for such stylish preparation. The end of one stroke must be the beginning of another—or the ball will be past you. As a result, the "setup" is the cocked position, with the racquet snapped behind the right ear for a forehand or the left ear for a backhand. There is a microsecond hesitation before the forward motion begins. That precious pause is the "setup."

Don't be alarmed if you never seem to have time to get into the "setup" position. The ball travels so fast and at such varying heights that it's impossible to get ready to strike every time in a systematic stance.

Racquetball's disadvantage is that the ball travels faster at closer quarters than in tennis, but it makes up for this handicap by it being nearly impossible to hit the ball out of court. A flail in tennis is a loser, while in racquetball it is part of many rallies—especially in the ranks below the pros.

Nonetheless, it is important to recognize when you have time to "setup" and take advantage of that moment. Balls that come off the back wall or that are the result of a rival's mishit are always susceptible to the "setup" position.

Forehand

The components of both forehand and backhand swing are similar. On the forehand, the shoulders turn clockwise together with the hips—pushing off from the left foot and pivoting on the right assist shoulder rotation. As the racquet is coiled above the right ear, the body weight is almost entirely on the back (right) foot, with the left foot pointing toward the front wall and only touching the floor for balance. Often the front foot hangs slightly in the air, waiting for the weight transfer from back to front foot. The body should face the sidewall at this stage of the stroke.

As the swing uncorks, the hips and shoulders now turn counterclockwise and will face the front wall on the follow-through. Watching the ball is crucial throughout the point—even more so than in tennis, where concentration can drift for a second with enough time to refocus on the ball without losing the point. Not knowing in racquetball where the ball is for even a fraction of a second can be disastrous. The ball moves too quickly to pick it up in midflight.

Depending on the amount of time you have, it is best to hit the ball as low to the floor as possible. A ball hit from chest high to a low front-wall target will bounce high as a result of the downward arc. A ball hit from ankle high straight ahead will more easily result in a near rollout with no bounce.

However, when the exchanges are zipping around the court like laser beams, you may have to hit a high bouncer or the ball will get away from you. In addition, you may not have time to execute shoulder rotation as a green missile streaks toward you. Don't fight it. Face the front wall straight on and flail. Marty Hogan's trademark is an open-stanced forehand thunderclap that does not suffer any loss of speed because classic form was not followed.

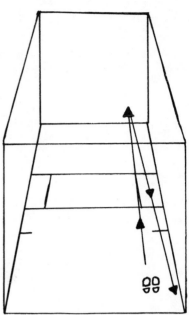

Forehand down-the-line pass

Brumfield's front foot hangs delicately as he begins weight transfer from right to left foot. His wrist is cocked and the racquet is coiled above his right ear. Charlie's eyes are riveted on the ball.

Brumfield makes contact midway
between knee and ankle.

The backhand is a mirror image of the forehand except that shoulder rotation is easier because in getting the racquet back the body turns naturally. The rotation is counterclockwise and the body faces the left sidewall at this moment. The racquet "setup" position is close behind the left ear, with the racquet face pointing upward toward the ceiling. The right shoulder dips slightly as the downswing begins, and, with the right foot now leading, weight transfers from the left to the front foot.

The follow-through of both forehand and backhand should show a stiff, straight right arm at the completion of the stroke no higher than the head. The trajectory of the racquet on both strokes starts head high and dips as low as reflexes allow—ankle high if possible and ends at the optimum shoulder height. Knees should be bent throughout—much lower than in tennis, for in racquetball there is a reward for hitting the ball from the shoetops straight ahead, while in tennis that same ball would go into the bottom of the net.

Because the forehand and backhand stroke must be triggered quickly, the racquet arm is released like a whip. In tennis, a player has the time and the luxury for an exaggerated backswing to build up a powerful forward motion gradually. But in racquetball, enormous speed must be generated quickly, which is why the backswing moves high in a coil position rather than straight back, where no whip-snap action is possible.

One important point: In order to prevent a long tennis-type swing, remember to lead both forehand and backhand swings with your elbow. This makes you cock your arm sharply at the elbow on the backswing, blocking the tendency to take the racquet straight back in time-wasting preparation.

Backhand

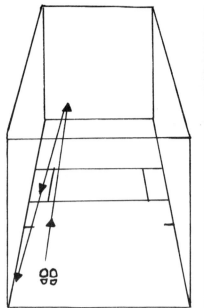

Backhand down-the-line pass

Brumfield's right shoulder dips as he coils racquet above left ear for backhand. The racquet face points toward ceiling.

Davey Bledsoe shows perfect form for weight transfer.

Bledsoe's backhand follow-through ends up almost head high.

The two most vital shots in racquetball are the serve and the return of serve. And of the two, the serve is even more crucial, since you can only win points when serving.

There are five basic serves: the drive, the garbage, the lob, the Garfinkle, and the reverse Garfinkle. Of these, the drive and the garbage should be used most often, with the Garfinkle or the lob resorted to only as a change of pace. The best position in which to stand for all serves is the middle of the service box, which is a nerve center for directing patterns of play. From the center you can serve to the forehand or backhand with equal deception, though 80 per cent of all serves should be aimed at the generally weaker backhand.

The ball must first be bounced on the floor within the service area and then smacked with your racquet at the front wall. It must carry past the short line (the back line of the service box) and land anywhere in the backcourt. It may hit either of the sidewalls (but not both) before bouncing but can't hit the back wall before hitting the floor. A ball not reaching the short line is a "fault" or a "short." A ball touching two walls or the back wall before bouncing is also a "fault" or a "long." Two faults result in a "handout," which means that your opponent becomes the server.

The drive serve is identical to the forehand stroke with the advantage that you control the ball bounce—not your opponent. The area of contact for the ball and racquet should be below the calf and sometimes as low as the ankletops when you feel your timing is magic. The sharp wrist snap is essential to impart enough speed so the ball does not pop up harmlessly. The target area for the drive serve is low (three feet or less) front wall. The ball bounds into the backcourt to the crease between the sidewall and floor about three to five feet past the short serve line. If you recognize that your service has less than blinding speed, aiming for the sidewall crack is a mistake. The best-percentage drive serve is one that misses the crack and continues almost to the back wall like a pass.

The drive serve should almost always be hit to the backhand or left side—certainly on every big point—with a quick delivery to the forehand used only for variation to prevent your foe from getting grooved. Since this serve involves violent motion causing both feet to move slightly, remember that no part of either foot may extend beyond the service zone until the served ball passes the short line. You can step on the service line but not beyond it.

The garbage serve is an effective shot for both beginner and expert, but should be particularly helpful to the novice because technique is not crucial. This half-lob serve should always be hit to the backhand—no exception—and begins with a waist-high bounce and a racquet hit with the strings almost parallel to the ceiling. The ball should hit the front wall higher than midway, continue upward, and arc a few feet over the server's head. It hopefully will touch the left sidewall five feet from the back wall, bounce once, and fall weakly in the corner. If properly executed, the only defense is a ceiling ball because it's impossible to generate power from a high backhand. You must guard against the gar-

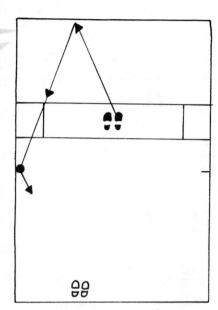

Drive serve

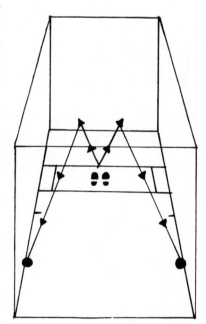

Path of drive serve to both forehand and backhand side

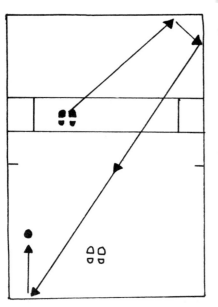

Path of two reverse Garfinkle serves

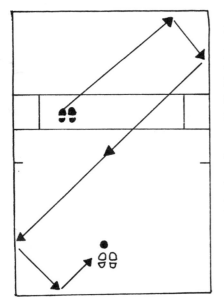

bage, serve dropping too short, which can be powdered by a low backhand after the bounce or carrying too far, which means a rebound off the back wall and a certain kill attempt by your foe. One more caution: A proper lob serve must brush the left sidewall, or your opponent will take the ball out of the air and smack it past you. (This shot is called a "fly kill.")

The server should always peek over his left shoulder to watch the retriever's plan. Don't turn your body to look, just your head, to get a jump on the next shot.

A sister serve to the garbage is the lob serve, the principal difference being the higher arc and the precision required for the lob to miss the ceiling and gently touch the left sidewall about eight feet from the back wall. The server should stand off center to the right of the service zone and follow through slightly more than on the garbage stroke. If deftly done, this serve frustrates your antagonist because the change of pace breaks the game's momentum. An opponent has more time to fret over his options with a lob serve, and the anxiety may unravel him completely. If imperfectly executed, the lob will result in a plum—ripe for the easy kill.

The crosscourt or reverse Z, or reverse Garfinkle serve, hits the front wall, then the right sidewall, caroms crosscourt, and bounces in front of the left rear sidewall. If you hit the ball closer to the junction between front wall and right sidewall, the ball will come straight back towards the back wall without hitting the left rear sidewall.

This serve requires endless experimentation to end up with exactly the right speed and direction to foil your opponent and probe his weakness. For example, how high or low on the front wall you aim the ball's first hit will ultimately affect the serve's speed and direction. The reverse Z is more effectively executed if the server stands to the left of center of the service box. But the further left you stand, the more you telegraph your intentions.

Novices have fun with the crosscourt serve, because they can have a good belt at a ball and make it land in their foe's backhand court. Warning: Be careful not to get hit by the ball after it strikes the sidewall on its way to the backcourt. You lose service immediately if the ball hits any part of your body.

The exact opposite of the reverse Z or reverse Garfinkle serve is the Z or Garfinkle. Charlie Garfinkle was a good—but not great—racquetball player who got a serve named after him by virtue of one stunning upset win over Charlie Brumfield in the 1971 nationals in Salt Lake City. Brumfield was not only the favorite for this tournament but was also considered by everyone to be the best player in the world—though he had yet to win a national singles title. Brumfield was blowing Garfinkle out, 21–8, and leading, 14–3, in the second game when Garfinkle started serving this weird Z ball to Brumfield's forehand at half speed. No one had ever served a Z to a man's strength before. Brumfield tried to drive the ball, but it came off the back wall as the score got closer and closer. Garfinkle won the match, 8–21, 21–20, 21–16, and forever won a unique place in the sport's history as the only man with a stroke that bears his name.

The Garfinkle serve should never be hit low and hard. The risks are too great for a crosscourt or down-the-line return kill. Yet as a change of pace at 50 per cent speed, it is a valuable variation.

In all the serving dialogue above, take note that the assumption is that two right-handed players are the protagonists. The instruction for a left-hander is exactly the reverse: The right court becomes the backhand side, the left court the forehand side, etc. Also, it may seem obvious, though I have never seen it mentioned before in any instruction books, the serve is always served with a forehand—rather than a backhand—stroke. I predict this will change one day, particularly with garbage, lob, and reverse Garfinkle serves, where deception, center-court vantage point, and improved angle may be accomplished from the backhand position.

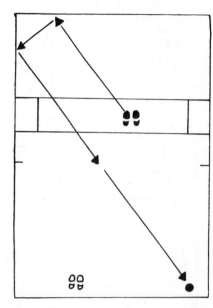

Garfinkle serve

Next to the serve, the return of serve is the most significant shot in racquetball. The proper position for the return is four feet from the back wall, since 80 per cent of all serves are directed to the backhand, it is prudent not to stand in the center of the court but a foot or so to the left of the center.

Because the percentages dictate that the serve will be fired down the left side, use the odds by preparing yourself with the backhand grip. Though what variety of return you use is controlled by the effectiveness of the serve, it is wise not to get bogged down with multiple choices. The ceiling ball should be your first selection. This shot has several advantages. First, it's an easy shot to execute, and the margin for error is large. In other words, you don't need a surgeon's precision to have the ceiling ball work efficiently.

The flight pattern of the ball is on a diagonal line to the ceiling about four feet from the front wall, down the front wall, bouncing around the service box, and continuing in a lazy arc to the backhand corner. The shot must be hit firmly enough not to hang temptingly in midcourt, begging for a kill attempt. A new danger has arisen with the trend toward an even more lively ball. A hard-hit ceiling ball now may rebound far enough off the back wall to invite an easy kill.

Since high backhands are more difficult to handle than high forehands, the ceiling ball should always be aimed down the left side. A perfectly executed ceiling ball hugs the left sidewall and is affectionately termed a "wallpaper ball."

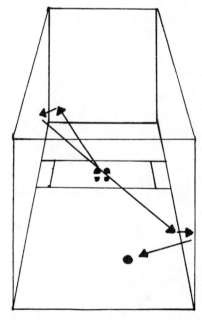

Alternate path of Garfinkle (or Z) serve

Not only does the ceiling-ball return have merit on its own as the safest shot, but it also has the additional advantage of moving your opponent from the sacred center-court position. The server has a distinct edge in being able to start at center court and score points outright while the receiver first has to win the right to serve. The server is also capable of squeezing off ace after ace with the fast ball, and so any maneuver to remove him from the center court is mandatory.

Ideally the ceiling-ball return will result in a ceiling-ball rally, which means that the server's edge has been dulled completely. Remember that

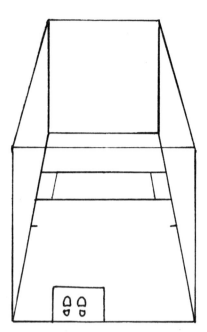

Position for service return is slightly away from back wall and to the left of center

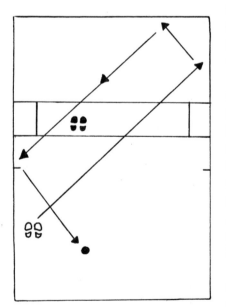

The Around-the-Wall return

just because the ceiling ball's path carries down the backhand side, it's not against the rules to take the ball on your forehand. It may mean that your left shoulder touches the left wall in order for you to get around for the shot, but it is worth it given the relative lack of strength in dealing with high backhands.

There is one psychological hangup about the ceiling-ball return—that it seems like a sissy shot. A beginner—and even many intermediate players—will think it's more *macho* to whack the return offensively. It's so much more tempting to wind up your whole body and let fly than to loft an undramatic defensive ceiling ball. This temptation highpoints that the discipline and patience involved in shot selection are just as important as shot execution.

The next service in priority ratings is the drive return. Again you must assume that every serve will be aimed at your backhand and therefore you can hold the racquet with a backhand grip. The drive return can be powdered down the line—first because you're keeping the ball on your rival's backhand side (presumably his weakness), and second because the distance to the front wall is shorter down the line than crosscourt. Your margin for error is therefore greater. Also ball speed will decrease slightly over the greater crosscourt distance and may hang the ball up precipitously in front of your opponent's forehand. A final reason for selecting down the line is that the server may not give you enough room to hit crosscourt.

Drive returns are executed in the same manner as the forehand and backhand drive—low off the front wall (three feet or less) and fast. The down-the-line return should come as close to the left sidewall without hitting it as possible and should die in the backhand corner. The ideal crosscourt return will strike the front wall to the right of center and penetrate deep into the forehand corner without hitting the right sidewall or back wall.

The next safest return is the Around-the-Wall Ball, which is a good response to a garbage or lob serve and can be used to force the server out of the strategic center-court area. The ball hits the sidewall first, then the front wall and the opposite sidewall and finally bouncing well past midcourt. The ATW Ball is easier to hit than the Z return, which must hit the front wall first, but is difficult to execute off a hard serve. The contact point for ball and racquet is waist high, and the first sidewall target area is halfway up the wall or higher. One of the purposes of the Around-the-Wall return is surprise, a factor that has been enhanced since the arrival of the fast ball. There is always the chance that a ball careening off the high walls at rocket speed will be just out of reach.

The kill return ranks near the bottom in logic. When you remember that the serve is the game's most offensive weapon, and that the kill is the most offensive ground stroke, how the two can combine is difficult to imagine. The kill smacks against the front wall so low and hard that it wins the point outright. The risk of the ball skipping (hitting the floor before the front wall) is great, and even if a near rollout is accomplished, the server is in the forecourt, the best possible position to retrieve a kill.

The only time the kill return should be contemplated is when a feeble serve bounces off the back wall. A weak server has forfeited his advantage, and you are obligated to complete his ruin by striking for the outright winner.

Two booby-prize returns for percentage are the lob and the Z ball. Both require perfect touch and timing and need inordinate time to execute. Rarely does the receiver have an abundance of time to ponder his options. Even if used as a response to the softer serves, there is always a better choice available (the Around-the-Wall Ball, for example, is far safer).

The lob can be any down-the-line shot but should almost always be aimed to your foe's backhand. It hits the front wall first halfway up or higher and arcs toward the backcourt, just missing the ceiling. It grazes the left sidewall and bounces around five feet past the short line and dies in the corner. If the lob is not perfectly hit, it will bounce short, inviting a sure rollout or else long—coming off the back wall at the right height and speed for a sitter.

The Z-ball return must hit the high front wall then sidewall without hitting the ceiling and bounce close to the back wall. If the receiver has enough time to attempt a Z ball, he certainly has enough time to try a higher percentage shot—either the drive or the Around-the-Wall Ball.

This is a strategic time to re-emphasize the importance of watching the ball. While it is essential never to take your eyes off the ball, there are countless difficult degrees of watching the ball. To understand this, you only need to half-volley a ball dropped from your hand to realize that you can actually hit the ball without looking at it. This is deceptive. Because a stroke can be completed without actually focusing on the ball, concentration can be lulled until the mind wanders into semi-attention. The first symptom of concentration loss is several mishits in a row, or a skip ball from a setup situation, or a ball getting beyond you that was not a perfect pass.

If there is a single time to reset your concentration dial, it is while waiting to receive serve. What you do on the first shot establishes the pattern for the entire exchange. Begin the rally weakly, and it is almost impossible to get back into it—given the natural advantage of the server. But marshaling all your attentive powers for a strong return will pay incredible dividends. For one thing, if you do make a respectable retrieve, the server may be frustrated that he has lost his built-in benefit.

Remember that the receiver must position himself at least five feet back of the short line and may not return the ball until it passes the short line. If you see a pumpkin serve waiting to be killed in the air, don't step into the service area or you'll lose the point.

One final observation: It can't be overemphasized that you should rely on the percentage shot. Your ego may be gratified by thrashing every return for the bottom board. It feels good to flail offensively at any ball within reach, but nonstop aggression may have zero in common with winning. It's your choice.

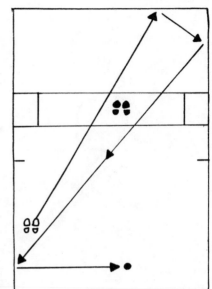

The Z-ball return

Bledsoe in intense concentration.

The overhead and volley, while requisite parts of the tennis player's arsenal, are not bread-and-butter shots in a racquetballer's repertoire. The reason is obvious. In tennis, if you pound a smash or forehand volley into the corner, it can't come back. But in racquetball the same shots may bounce harmlessly off the back wall ready for the kill.

The volley and overhead can be effective against beginners and intermediates because the ball speed may be bewildering. But you can see that if the ultimate shot is hard and low, both volley and overhead flight paths travel in a high-to-low line, meaning a high bounce easy to retrieve.

Some balls are moving so slowly through the air that they can be taken in flight low to the floor and with a full swing just like a drive. This is not

Bledsoe swing—volleys at a low ball to his forehand.

a typical volley situation, though technically any ball hit before bouncing is a volley.

Even the experts hit volleys and overheads when they are forced to. In other words, in a rapid rally situation, a ball plucked out of the air may be better than the alternative—which is having the shot get away totally. Or an overhead may be a better choice than having a lob die without rebound in the corner. Percentages dictate that overheads be hit cross-court, touching the sidewall first to reduce the shot's speed and lessen the chance for a plumb off the back wall or sidewall. It is ironic that these two shots, which are the most offensive weapons in tennis, are used almost entirely defensively in top-grade racquetball.

Brumfield's "setup" for the overhead is flawless.

A critical element in improving your racquetball skill is shot selection. Analyze instantly whether the situation demands a defensive or offense stroke and don't compromise your choice. In other words, don't strike a pass at half speed. The most common situation for offense is when the

Brumfield's overhead is the most feared in the game.

ball bounces off the back wall. Not only is there time for a pass or kill attempt with a slow rebound off the back wall, but also, since you are deep in the backcourt and your opponent occupies the vital center-court area, a bold stroke is needed to force him out of center.

A helpful tip to footwork in back-wall play: Don't plant your feet too firmly as you prepare the swing, else you misjudge the ball's bounce. Small steps toward the front wall as you begin your windup help continue your forward motion. It's not improper to shuffle the feet forward a few inches during the stroke itself if it looks as if the ball might get away from you. Most footwork mistakes off the backwall are the result of having to lunge forward at the ball because it is moving away from the body toward the front wall. The back-wall ball is the only shot that does not come toward you, so a rigid "setup" position may leave you off balance as the ball scoots away from your swing.

It is imperative to position yourself in center court, and soon as you make a retrieve deep in the backcourt to fight for the center court again. This vantage point is located directly between the sidewalls and a stride in back of the short line.

Strictly playing the odds, the center-court posts is the shortest distance to every shot in racquetball. There is no other position that gives you a better head start in any direction.

The shortest distance means quicker time to get there and, just as important, less energy spent in doing so. For a single point this may not seem important, but over an entire match if you have to circle an opponent controlling center court for every retrieve, you're covering three times the territory.

Not only is center court the best position to defend any shot, but it is also the optimum place to direct an offensive attack as well. The farther you move away from the center the more limited your stroke options are. Certainly the velocity of your stroke is much greater when shot twenty-one feet from the front wall than from thirty-six feet in the backcourt.

The server starts off in control of the center-court area, and he should relinquish his headquarters only when chased into the corner. But if you're not serving, how do you recapture the center? The ceiling-ball return is one method, and the Around-the-Wall Ball is another. Obviously if you attempt a kill and make it, you regain serve instantly, but the risks of skipping the ball or leaving a setup are enormous. The crosscourt and down-the-line drives, if hit perfectly, will certainly force the server out of the sacred center area, but if he anticipates quickly he'll leave you struggling in the backcourt.

The server, on the other hand, should use all his skill to maintain center court. In addition to the ready-made advantages of serving—surprise and its near-kill potential—the server has the opportunity to probe a foe's weakness unmercifully.

The server can start the action by attacking an understrength stroke and never let up except for variation. Despite comments to the contrary, a player's weakness will not become his strength in the course of one match.

Center-Court Strategy

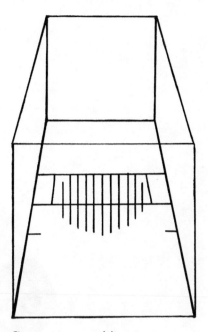

Center-court position

A rare moment with Brumfield on the defensive. He is in an impossible retrieving position and instead of going for the bold low percentage pass, he floats a lob, hoping to give him time to get back into position. The lack of wrist snap tells that this is not a ceiling-ball attempt.

There is only one method for practice in racquetball that is worth mentioning: the solo drill. There are conventional techniques where your partner serves an entire game and then the roles switch and he receives for twenty-one points. This exercise focuses on total offense or total defense over a protracted period. Or having a partner hit to your weakness for fifteen-minute sessions. But the solo drill is so crucial to the development of every player—from beginner to expert—that all other training devices seem incidental.

The solo drill has countless advantages over other improvement exercises. You can spend as much time as you want working on your problem without dividing the effort to solve someone else's. There is always a temptation in a partnership drill to practice for a while and then play. Competition is not practicing. If you are working on an improved shot and then decide to play a few games, as soon as the match gets close, you'll revert to your old techniques in order to win. As a result your new shot won't get a chance to develop.

The most often used solo drill is the drop and kill, where you drop the ball in front of your foot (right foot for backhand, left foot for forehand) while facing the sidewall. Let the ball drop to the middle of the calf and fire at the front wall. When working on one particular stroke—the forehand kill from the backcourt, for example—try to keep all the conditions identical: height of ball at moment of contact, distance from the front wall, distance from the sidewall. Don't try one forehand from the service box and another from a foot from the back wall. And *don't* vary the height from the floor at which you hit the ball. Do multiple repetitions of the same stroke from the same position, same height, etc. Then change court positions for the next drill and perform identical repetitions.

Maximum efficiency for this drill is accomplished by allowing no variation within the single stroke practiced. It should be emphasized not to rally with yourself during this practice. Strike the ball once from the optimum stance, then pick up the ball and start over. The concept here is for the pattern to be repeated so many times that when you face the exact ball location in match conditions, you don't have to think about execution. Instinct will take over and direct your body movement.

In carrying out the drop-and-kill drill, you must think of your brain as a memory bank that scores the image of the 10,000 or so hits it takes to develop a single stroke. In actual competition, the ball travels too fast for you to give oral instructions to your arm—such as, "extend the racquet way back," "lock your wrist," "keep your elbow close to the body." Retrieving information from the brain on how to execute comes in the form of an "automatic pilot" device. If you have cranked enough stroke patterns into the mind, the correct information will pop out automatically.

You can imagine the various solo-drill variations from the drop and kill. An easy back-wall practice is to toss the ball on the floor toward the back wall and then hit as it comes off the back wall. An alternative to this is to throw the ball directly against the back wall and strike it after the bounce, or, standing in one corner, pitch the ball so it bounces back wall, sidewall, and floor—and then hit.

Brumfield practices forehand drop-and-kill routine.

The overhead can be practiced by smashing the ball so it hits the floor in front of the front wall and bounces high for another overhead. This exercise is primarily to build up overhead strength—not accuracy—and has the benefit of not having to fetch the ball after each hit.

One innovation for the solo drill should be helpful and time-saving. Instead of bringing one ball into the practice court, bring twenty-five (collect old tournament balls that have been rejected as "dead") in a shopping bag and place it close to each practice stance. In this way no time or energy is wasted picking up the balls after every swing.

1. The ceiling return enables you to neutralize the normal advantage of the server or of the man controlling the strategic center-court area. To work percentages for you, the ceiling ball should be paramount in your mind during shot selection. The ceiling ball is not as much fun to hit as the kill attempt or the Z ball, but statistically it's the soundest without question.

2. Remember that there are many levels of keeping your eye on the ball, and that you may not know that your concentration is gradually slipping because you *can* hit the ball without looking directly at it. A simple device for retraining your attention is to try to see the ball's label as it whizzes by. You certainly won't succeed on photon streakers, but the exercise will succeed in reviving your concentration.

3. The best shot off the back wall is the kill attempt. The percentages are finally with you on this go-for-broke stroke, and your *macho* ego, which has agonized over hitting ceiling balls, can at least be satisfied.

4. Experimenting is not evil. As you read various instruction books and listen to various professionals, take advice as a guide—as a tool for exploring certain parameters of technique. For example, don't be afraid to choke up on the racquet handle no matter what you hear.

5. Concentration. You're going to be on the court for an hour or more, so why let any distraction occur? Try focusing on every shot as if it were match point. From this exercise, you'll discover that your concentration still fluctuates on every point. The fear of losing the final point does activate extra concentration chemistry.

6. Anger. There is no such thing as an easy shot in racquetball. What the sport's crybabies don't realize is that what they consider to be an "off day" may truly represent their game. And those rare occasions when they shoot winner after winner off the bottom board may really be their "off day."

In any event, a blind rage has never yet recouped a lost point, and it may well effect your ability to function properly for future points.

7. The solo drill, which is considered unchic in tennis (hitting against the backboard), is mandatory for improvement in racquetball. Figure that if you're a good athlete, it will take approximately 1,000 drop-and-kill shots (1½ hours) to groove a single shot. As a result of this solitary drilling, *playing will become an extension of practice.*

8. Percentages. Play the percentages even in practice. For example, if you want to practice your return of serve, the majority of your practice session should be spent on the backhand-return serve, since 80 per cent of all serves will be aimed down the backhand side. By the way, the best-percentage kill shot hits the sidewall first, then the front wall.

9. The server should retreat two steps on a diagonal toward the direction of his serve. This manuever will screen off some of your opponent's shot options. There are fine lines among blocking, intimidation, and percentage positioning. The best example of this tight definition is the back of the legs of the three random touring pros. Shannon Wright and Steve

Brumfield executes a ceiling-ball
return.

Strandemo both crowd, and their legs are a quiltwork of orange bruises.
Yet Steve Keeley stays out of everyone's way, and his legs are pink and
unscarred. It's probably impossible to be precise about the difference between blocking and strategic stance—just so long as you know there is a
difference.

10.   Stretching. There are endless books on conditioning, and if our
purpose here was to get you in perfect shape we'd need another volume.
But basically most of the exercise theories are a matter of emphasis—how
much running, how much weight work, and how much stretching.

   Since 99.9 per cent of those who read this book are not on the racquetball tour and have other jobs, my advice is simple: It is far better for
overall conditioning to spend thirty minutes every day exercising or

Brumfield continues to apply his
laser beam focus on the ball!

playing racquetball, than playing racquetball for two hours every three
days. With regular exercise every day, the body does not risk the shock
of exhaustion or muscle strain.

The most important element in the exercise program is stretching. A
full fifteen minutes in the morning spent stretching and another fifteen
minutes in the evening will prevent more injuries than two hours of
racquetball practice. A simple stretching routine involves rotating the

neck back and forth ten times; turning the shoulders clockwise and counterclockwise ten times; rotating the waist (trunk) right and left ten times; and finally stretching your fingers toward your toes—point toes up simultaneously—and then bend your knees and grab the back of your heel. It is not even necessary to keep your knees straight when trying to touch your toes.

And finally lie on your back and bring your legs straight up over your head and hold them there until it hurts or you get bored, whichever comes first.

For the part-time athlete, stretching is far more critical to conditioning than abstract exercise or playing. Even for the touring pro, stretching should be regarded just as seriously as his practice session or he may not be able to finish his practice session.

Ninety-nine per cent of all racquetball played is singles. This statistic on first inspection might be considered a deterrent to the sport's ultimate growth. Tennis encourages the tandem game to the extent that an estimated 70 per cent of the sets played are doubles. In golf, over 85 per cent of the pairings are foursome.

The team element is an enormous attraction for both sports. Yet while the appeal of the camaraderie in a partnership is obvious, the characteristics of the doubles game may actually detract from its appeal. Two sets of tennis doubles are not much exercise. Each man covers approximately half the court he would in singles, and because of the emphasis on serve and volley, there is virtually no premium on running ability.

In racquetball or tennis singles, however, a tremendous boost is given to the player with foot speed—even more so in racquetball, where your quickness is always rewarded, while the technical side of tennis must be mastered before agility will pay dividends. Therefore, for young people who want exercise and want it fast both on the court and in their learning curve, racquetball singles has extraordinary appeal.

There is a further discouraging word to be said for racquetball doubles, and that is the inherent danger of four rambunctious athletes moving about an area forty feet by twenty feet by twenty feet armed with metal clubs. The potential for eye and face injuries is serious, and if you're too *macho* to wear an eyeguard in singles, going on the court without eye protection in doubles is insanity.

The characteristics that make racquetball so appealing to participants —quick learning time and rapid exercise—do not gain benefits in doubles and, in fact, lose some ground in terms of less exercise and the hazard factors. Furthermore, no matter how artistic the arguments are for the excitement of doubles competition to spectators, the logic breaks down when one realizes that fans cherish *mano a mano* confrontations. Even in tennis, where journalists for years have harped on the superiority of doubles over singles as a spectator sport, too much is made of the drama of high-speed exchanges among four men at net. The point is that the principal viewing thrill is the duel itself between two men or women where a single winner must emerge—not necessarily the speed of the action itself. Boxing, wrestling, horse racing, and the Olympics are competitions that emphasize the gladiator nature of the contest.

For example, it is not good enough to run a world-record 3-minute mile if you finish second to a speedster who is clocked in 2:58. But if you won the world heavyweight boxing title without performing up to par, it would be deemed more of an accomplishment than fighting a brilliant fight but getting knocked out in the fifteenth round.

One more thing: Commercial sponsors want to post the highest prize possible for one winner alone because it highlights the accomplishment of a single champion. Players' unions in both golf and tennis have struggled for years to spread the purse out more evenly all the way down to first-round losers and even to golfers who don't make the cut. On the other hand, sponsors insist they need a giant first-place check to trumpet the event's importance. It is felt this is accomplished better with one fifty-thousand-dollar check to Jimmy Connors or Jack Nicklaus than with fifty one-thousand-dollars checks spread among an entire field.

If this seems a belabored belittling of doubles, there is a reason. We are all creatures of custom, and sometimes the custom should be questioned —like the one that says doubles is a better game than singles. Well, racquetball is not traditionbound and is not embarrassed to exclaim that singles is a better sport. Racquetball superstar Steve Keeley concludes, "No more than two people should occupy one court at one time." He advises that there should be posted above every racquetball court entrance a sign like the fire-hazard sign: "Capacity, Two Persons."

There still may be times, for one reason or another, that you may be called on to play doubles, and the following information should be helpful.

Because only half the territory has to be covered in singles as in doubles, the tandem game requires more patience and control. The kill shot is used sparingly and at the shooter's peril because there are two foes ready to track down the attempted winner and pound it back if it is not right on the mark. As a result, the typical rally in doubles is a ceiling-ball exchange interrupted only by the impatience of one of the four players who drives to break the tempo. Quickly the other team tries a rollout which, failing will be killed ending the rally.

The most common doubles formation is the side-by-side method, with the stronger player on the left side and the weaker player on the right. This assumes that the better player has the better backhand, leaving opponents the option of directing play to the weaker man's forehand— which should be his strength—playing down the middle, which is controlled by the stronger man's forehand or to his backhand side—also superior. In this way all corners of the court are protected from weakness.

A less common formation is the front-and-back pattern—affectionately known as the "I" formation, which, unlike tennis, is not a rude commentary on a team's lack of doubles sense. As it suggests, this style has one man in front court who is the retriever and his partner, who should have a keenly developed ceiling game, in backcourt.

In practice, a combination of the I formation and side-by-side may be the ideal composite, with the more agile player positioned close to the service area with a prearranged assignment for the front man to take all short kills.

The essential strategy of doubles is to occupy center court when it is not your turn to hit the ball. The team that has just made a hit has the unwritten right to control the center court and can do so until it is their turn to hit when the center position must be relinquished.

Performed properly, doubles play will result in a perpetual flow of traffic to and from the center-court sweet spot, though more often the exchange resembles a bumper-car mashing of elbows and shoulders.

If the urge to break up the ceiling-ball montage becomes too tempting, the best kill percentage shot is the sidewall, front-wall pinch. This ball shoots short off the front wall and is difficult to retrieve, and even if it is mishit, it is not apt to sit up for a return kill.

Another strategy to beat the monotony of the ceiling-ball rally is the standard V-ball pass, which caroms from dead center off the front wall to a deep right- or left-sidewall angle. Drive serves and low Garfinkle and "Z" serves are far more important in doubles than the lob or garbage delivery. Since both the server and his partner must remain in the service box until the serve passes the short line, the slower serves don't generate the confusion that the fast drives accomplish.

Not to hit a forcing serve in doubles is to lose the natural advantage of being the side to initiate that confusion. In first-flight doubles competition, the service return must not only rarely be missed but should be played either with a mind to putting the opposing team on the defensive or to retreating to the defensive with a ceiling ball. No middle ground.

Because of the crowded court, some shots—ineffective in singles—can be devastating in doubles. For instance, any ball that can be taken in the air should be volleyed. There is an atmosphere of bedlam in doubles, and snappy half volleys and volleys add to the congestion.

A standard tactic employed in doubles is to pour the attack on the weaker player. This isolation technique is effective in racquetball, where it is not necessary for the server to alternate serves to his opponent. After the lesser man is ground down it may be fortuitous to switch the attack briefly to the stronger man, who may miss because he has been removed from the rhythm of the action. Once the dominant member of the team becomes unbuttoned, the partnership dissolves.

One of the principal reasons for playing doubles at all is that occasionally there are too many players for the courts available and doubling up lets everybody play. Another reason is that the veterans feel that singles is too taxing and somewhere they read that after forty you should only play doubles.

Both are products of lopsided reasoning. If the doubles game is awful, don't force it. If court space is a valid complaint, why not three per team and six on a court? (Not so ridiculous as it sounds. An early pioneer of paddleball describes "cutthroat doubles"—six players on a court—with relish.) In any case, a crowd of six makes just as little sense as four monsters pounding away at the ball (and at each other) in a space that is big enough only for two. If there are still doubles fanatics listening, they should carry the cudgels to the racquetball fathers and insist the doubles court be constructed larger, as in squash, hard racquets, or tennis.

As for the veterans who think doubles is less taxing than singles, they're probably right insofar as the fatigue factor is concerned. But the injury level—eye lacerations, waffle face, and leg welts—ranks alongside mayhem in danger, and outside of a racquetball court such conduct would subject the offender to arrest for criminal assault.

Within the eye of the racquetball tempest that rages wildly around the country, there is a smaller storm—women's racquetball—that fuels the larger frenzy. It's easy to see why. Ninety-eight per cent of all American squash facilities are located at men's clubs, prep schools, and colleges. Women are tolerated as either a throwaway bone to women's rights or as a critical source of income to financially desperate clubs. Because squash courts are male chauvinist bastions, only twenty thousand of the five hundred thousand squash players in America are women. Yet because women are greeted with more enthusiasm in racquetball than the snicker or sneer reserved for lady squash players, there are fully one million female racquetball players out of a total three million.

The fact that women played tennis on a wholesale basis before 1968 was an accident rather than a conscious effort to encourage their participation. Ninety per cent of all private tennis clubs in America were primarily men's clubs, with wives allowed in as part of the husband's membership. Even today at some of the poshest clubs in the land, women are still technically not voting members. At one exquisite club on Long Island, for example, ladies are permitted under a quaint proviso called "annual subscriber," where for a one-hundred-dollar reduction in dues the women have the same privileges as the men except voting rights. These chauvinist anachronisms are throwbacks to an eighteenth-century era when women were regarded as chattels—with severe restrictions on owning real estate or inheriting property. Remember that the Nineteenth Amendment, giving women the right to vote, wasn't passed until 1920.

Racquetball didn't have to cross rough history to grant equal rights to women. They were an integral part of its growth and success from the beginning. When the construction of racquetball court clubs began in 1973, women were welcomed hungrily as a principal source of revenue for nonprime periods in the morning and afternoon. The business logic was that the housewife had free time when their husbands were at work. The indoor tennis industry first recognized use patterns of women in the late 1960s, but there still was a difference between the interest level of a female racquetball player and that of a tennis player.

Tennis is too difficult for women to learn quickly. They can't truly enjoy the game until they've learned to rally, which takes almost two years. They can love the chitchat, the coffee afterward, and especially the cute outfits, but a beginner's affection for tennis is social, not athletic. Some tennis manufacturers make ladies' warm-up suits that will never be used for tennis—like the jacket with a hood—but for leisure-time flopping about instead.

Interest in ladies tennis leagues and ladies doubles proliferated in the 1970s. But there was also a large degree of phantom love for tennis. What many men and women love about tennis is the loving itself—like the writer who likes the image of being a writer and is not particularly turned on to having to write every day for a living.

There is no fake ritual about liking racquetball because of its fancy image. The women play because they want to play. And because racquetball does not take extraordinary skill to pop a few up against the front wall and start a rally, the women don't get discouraged by their

The women.

inability to learn the game right away. Yet in tennis or golf there is enormous turnover at the beginner level because the players get discouraged at their apparent ineptness. On the other hand, once a racquetballer is turned on, she won't quit.

There is a question whether racquetball will appeal to masses of women in the thirty-five-to-fifty age bracket, because while the sport is simple to learn, there is a premium placed on running and physical conditioning. Neither tennis—with its emphasis on doubles—nor golf are more strenuous than a country walk. If middle-aged women ever determine that fitness is critical to their lives, the explosion of racquetball could be tremendous. Racquetball will never appeal to women who want to dazzle by their chic appearance. Racquetball will always be a game of shorts, not pleated, high-fashion dresses. But there are an enormous number of women who find this lack of show and pretense appealing.

Tennis will continue to be extremely expensive for women; a racquetball court costs $70,000 to construct, but a single tennis court costs close to $150,000. The cost difference is paid for by the player. For example, an average racquetball court club charges $35 to join and $5.00 per hour to play, while a comparable indoor tennis facility would have no annual fee but charge $15 per hour. There are enormous variations to these figures, depending on location, with the top court club hourly fee reported in Detroit at $12 per hour and the highest indoor tennis time charged in New York City at $55 an hour. The best recorded bargain in the land is the Odessa Texas family YMCA, where for $115 per year a family can play racquetball all day, every day. There is no equivalent bargain in tennis.

The million women racquetball players are hard-core, no-nonsense athletes. Their numbers will grow staggeringly as racquetball supplies the obvious answer for women who want exercise, want it fast, cheap, with no frills required.

The most appealing feature of racquetball for women is that they excel at it. In fact, a women can match skills with a man in racquetball far easier than in any other sport. Upper body strength is not required to hit a racquetball hard. Power comes from form and timing. In addition, the court is small, and so a blinding sprinter's speed is not as important as anticipation and a good pair of eyes.

Most women athletes—pro or amateur—are labeled inferior in both isolated judgment and in stark comparison to men. In golf, the ladies' tees are placed far in front of the men's to patronize a wife's inability to hit the ball as far as her husband. In social mixed doubles, it is considered impolite to whap an ace or a chest-high volley at your lady opponent. Raw strength and speed are important in many sports, and so the contrast in abilities between male and female athletes is vivid, and yet generates heated arguments. The women pros will argue that talent should be measured by standards other than calibrations in seconds or yards. Style should be accorded recognition and, more importantly, entertainment value should be rewarded on its own merits regardless of speed or power. These arguments have aided the women's rights movement in sports incredibly. Racquetball may not need the help of such ethereal logic.

The idea that a man and woman might compete in the same arena, in the same sport, and be judged by the same standard is a dramatic departure from the propaganda spread by both men and women in the past. Though there is no mixed competition in racquetball, the evidence collected so far supports the position that there is relative equality in the ability of the sexes.

Many supportive arguments for the women come from an unlikely source: the men. Steve Keeley, a senior citizen among the racquetball superstars, an author, and discerning analyst of player styles, is convinced that "the top ten women pros are on the same level with 'A' group of men." And further that "Peggy Steding or Shannon Wright [the top two women in the game] would beat Steve Mondry [who ranked No. 12 in the early 1977 prize-money listing]. In fact, I think Steve and Shannon played on a bet. I don't know who won, but if Mondry did, it would have been his ego alone that kept him going." Peggy Steding was more conclusive. "If I was playing good I could hold my own against Mondry. I play better against the men than against women. The first few years I ever played, I competed mainly in the men's division. Naturally I started in B tournaments but wound up in the A's. Never finished below third in any event I ever entered—men included."

Shannon herself was even more positive. "I do play Mondry and beat him 21–10 generally."

Steve Strandemo (third-ranking man player in the same listing) was gentlemanly enough to concede that he did play Shannon Wright and split games with her. He admitted, "I was hobbling, and it was before I was really feeling better. But she hit the ball really good. I *was* practicing, mind you. I took one type of serve and used it for the whole hour without diversifying serves or returns. I can't say what the outcome would be if I played the points like they were part of a match. I know she'd score a few."

Shannon responded abruptly, "Strandemo and Keeley are both control players. I hit the ball harder than either of them and more consistently too. It's not unusual for me to win games from these guys."

It's an astonishing dialogue. It would be as if Ilie Nastase, whose flowing black mane reminds one of Strandemo, said at a similar stage in his career when he ranked No. 3 in the world and Chris Evert was the best that she would do well against him. That if he were not feeling great she'd split sets with him. It simply wouldn't happen in tennis, but the analogy is useful when trying to evaluate the relative abilities of the men and the women. The analogy is also important when examining the reason why racquetball is so popular with women. It is well known that the game is simple to learn at the beginner's level, but now there's the additional encouragement that a woman's potential skills are not held back by lack of physical strength.

The court-club operators recognize that the women are a critical source of income in the off hours and cater to them as a result by offering spacious locker rooms, saunas, jacuzzi baths, and nursery rooms for their children.

The decor of court clubs is obviously aimed not only at men. There are attractive lounges with giant television sets, reading areas, and long, comfortable sofas. The atmosphere is not the conventional staid setting of a men's club. The clubs are consciously selling the theme of a mixed membership. It's almost like a singles bar—substituting a racquetball court for the bar. Make no mistake about it: There is an element of gentle sexuality in the surroundings. Both the men and the women are aware of the mixed element, and they like it. A far cry from many English clubs, where the mere appearance of a lady inside the corridors would horrify a British clubber.

Because glass courts encourage a gallery even for a friendly game, the women become a part of the spectator scene too. Most competitors play best with an audience—it aids concentration—and pros and amateurs interviewed at twelve court clubs in Florida and San Diego all said they preferred to have someone watch—even if it was only one person. Generally there was a feeling that a club where men and women shared their sport was far more dynamic than an exclusively male establishment.

The historical difference between racquetball and other sports is that racquetball never took women for granted. The women were an integral part of the game's growth from its inception.

Even at the professional level, the women did not have to wait a long apprenticeship period—for the men to make a healthy living—before they were given their own pro tour.

National Racquetball Club's Bob Kendler had enormous vision when he diverted prize money from the men's game to a women's circuit. He believed that since women were such a vital part of developing the sport overall, they should have a chance to create top stars for their amateur participants to emulate. He was particularly convinced that his gesture was proper when several of the leading men pros became unsporting and rowdy in tournament matches, which he feared would frighten off the fledging sponsors that he had wooed so cautiously at the beginning of professionalism. Injecting prize money into women's tournaments was a way to hedge Kendler's bet by offering companies participation in the broad base of the game's future.

Not everyone agreed with Kendler's generosity. The world's No. 1, Charlie Brumfield, objected. "I think it's a mistake to divert prize money from the men to the women's division at this time. Other sports waited until the men's tour was on solid footing, and at least the best sixteen players in the nation were earning a living. From my observations, spectators and the media are interested first in the top men professionals and the women pros afterward. Nothing against the touring women. They try and train as hard as anyone else, but I don't think we should run a five-ring circus until we can run one ring properly financed and successful overall."

Steve Keeley dissented from Brumfield's summary. "The success of racquetball is due to the women. Without them we'd be a notch down the scale. They aren't as much fun to watch and couldn't go on tour by themselves. No one would be interested. They have to tour with us now. It's fine. The money taken out of the men's game is a small sacrifice for what the women are contributing."

Peggy Steding and Shannon Wright are the two best women racquetball players in the world. They represent the opposite ends of the tour and women's racquetball. Peggy is forty-one and a hard-nosed athlete.

Shannon Wright.

Shannon is twenty-one and is the strong, silent type. Peggy didn't start out as a racquetball player—in fact, she didn't even begin playing until she was thirty-five. She was a ranking sectional player who was looking for more action than tennis was able to provide in her hometown, Odessa, Texas.

She's not afraid of shooting a ball up an opponent's backside if the going gets sticky, while many of the other pros are simply too polite. Her jet-black hair looks as if it has been waxed to keep it in place on the court, but she doesn't care if she looks stylish so long as she wins. Peggy Steding has been playing racquetball for only six years, and after just two years was the national champion. She held the title for four successive years until Shannon Wright began to challenge her domination in 1977.

Steding is a good spokeswoman for her sex. Her personal example helps put to rest the two greatest deterrents for any woman starting sports: the fear of being too old to play and the fear of not being good enough to play. Not everyone can be Peggy Steding, but when she talks it makes sense to listen.

"The big plus for women's racquetball is that it's easy to pick up. You don't have to be really good to enjoy it. Any woman can get in there and pitty-pat the ball around and still have fun," Steding offers.

As far as the worry that racquetball may not be a middle-aged woman's game, Steding is also comforting. "If a female stays healthy, she can play forever. Conditioning is obviously a factor, but I don't even have the discipline to run, and I'm in good shape. Part of the reason I can play all day is that I concentrate well. If I can beat someone 21–5 or 21–6 I'm going to beat 'em that. I don't piddle-diddle around with them." With a twenty-five-year background of playing tennis—she still gives lessons in the summer—Peggy provided cogent arguments for a woman to pick one sport over the other.

"Even if you're blessed with talent, tennis is frustrating for women beginners. All you do is chase balls, and there are no rallies. On the other hand, racquetball is not hard to pick up at all. And as far as a workout, there is no comparison. When I started playing racquetball, I was still playing tennis tournaments in Texas as well as competing in an industrial basketball league. I thought I was in shape. I played three games of racquetball and my tongue was hanging out."

She thinks that by the end of the 1980s racquetball may overtake tennis. "When you see women give up teaching tennis and go into racquetball, you know something is up. Furthermore, from a spectator's point of view, there's no contest. Racquetball is much more exciting. You really get engrossed watching two good women play racquetball. When you watch good women play tennis it could put you to sleep."

One of the elements that adds to the ability of women to excel at racquetball is concentration. Because the ball travels so fast at short distances, a mind that focuses on the ball like a fist—not letting up until the point is over—will dominate. Psychologists have told us for years that women deal with stress far better than men. It follows that since a competitive battle presents a typical high-stress situation, women will find a way to resolve the tension and ultimately concentrate better than men.

Peggy Steding put it another way. "I've played guys with a lot more strength than me but who couldn't bust an egg hitting the ball. Maybe they were tense playing a girl, I don't know. But power in racquetball comes from timing. Once your timing is down, anticipation—besides concentration—is 80 per cent to 90 per cent of the game. A lot of times it doesn't matter how fast you are. If you don't get the jump on the ball by anticipating it, you're not going to get there anyway."

Steding's contagious spirit about her sport is remarkable. She is enthusiastic about racquetball's growth potential and points to women's sports generally being on the upgrade as accelerating the popularity of racquetball.

"Court-club owners will tell you that if it weren't for the women, the clubs couldn't stay open. The women fill the slack of the day. The best sign of how these owners are catering to women is that the smart ones are putting in nurseries so the housewives can play and not worry about the kids," Steding declared.

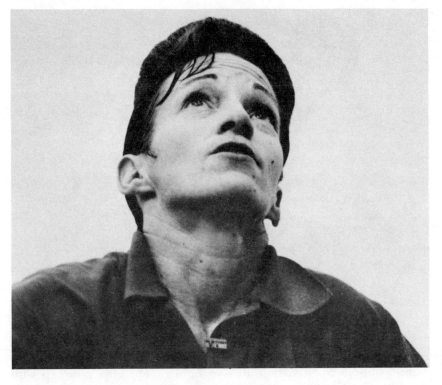

Peggy Steding appeals to the referee.

Shannon Wright has been playing seriously since she was seventeen. She moved to San Diego from Dallas in order to become the best player in the land. She lives oncourt and thinks about little else but racquetball.

Strandemo confirmed Shannon's chances to become a superstar: "She'll make it. She wants it bad."

Shannon's confidence is apparent from the start. When commenting on Steding's and her own ability to compete with many of the top men pros, Shannon spurted, "Peggy could never beat any of the guys like I could." But she adds quickly, "When I play some amateur men who crunch the ball, I can't win."

Shannon shreds the theory that older pros can compete with young athletes. "There are exceptions," she offers. "Peggy Steding is the most exceptional athlete I've ever encountered, but she's unusual. Even Peggy has slowed down enormously over the past year. And it's age."

But that doesn't mean racquetball has no allure for the masses. "Racquetball can be played by anybody," Shannon points out. "Amateurs can seek any level of competition they want to. I used to teach at Texas Christian University in Fort Worth and had a guy who joined my class at sixty-nine years old. He's now seventy-two, and he's still having a blast. When you get past forty your reaction time and reflexes may slow down, but that's only important for the top pros, who constitute less than 1 per cent of the game."

"Older people love to get in there and get a workout," she continued. "They enjoy the social part being around younger people and all."

Shannon does not strike feminist chords when she announces, "It's easier for men to learn the game than women because women don't learn

Shannon Wright takes a time out.

basic hand-eye co-ordination at a young age. The guys grow up with football and Little League baseball and learn those physical skills early."

"But women can enjoy racquetball just as much as the men," she counters. "It's terrific exercise for housewives who can take off when their kids are at school. They can stay in shape—not get flabby—and socialize with their girlfriends. Besides, it's an inexpensive way to have fun."

Shannon's attitude on male and female roles seems inconsistent, but when it comes to her personal racquetball career, she doesn't waver an eyelash.

"I love the fact that the men's and women's pro circuits are combined," she says. But when asked if she dated anyone on the men's tour, Shannon exploded. "Are you kidding? No chance."

"There's a very small and tight-knit group playing pro racquetball and most of the good players work for Leach Industries. If we started dating the men, rumors would fly like a Z ball. It would make everyone goofy. So we keep it all on a business basis."

Then with steam shooting from her eyes, she concluded with a one-liner that would make feminists duck: "The only people I practice with are the men. It's the only way I can get competition."

If a frenetic cult of racquetball does exist, the question arises whether there is an epicenter to the cult, whether there is a white-hot core that fuels the fanaticism that slowly rolls over our land. Like the opposite forces of a magnet, there is an irresistible attraction for all pro racquetball players to make San Diego their home base, and at the same time the city's resident superstars shoot a beaconlike signal to every court club in the country.

San Diego is the mecca of racquetball. There is a suspicion that Californians think California is the mecca of the universe, so their self-serving accolades are not given much credibility. But Californians had nothing to do with associating San Diego with racquetball, and, indeed, among sportsmen in Los Angeles, Newport Beach, and San Francisco, there is not widespread recognition for racquetball being anything special. You see, the Golden State has so much fun and games to choose from in the form of golf, tennis, surfing, sailing, and swimming that making an extra fuss over one of them is like forcing a *bon vivant* to be a vegetarian.

Nonetheless, there is a reason for racquetball's pulsating circles around San Diego. Californians have an image of being incredibly outdoorsy. They are by virtue of their citizenship considered to be athletic and healthy. The environment emphasizes a strong physical culture, whether it be for professional or recreation athletes, and a businessman is not embarrassed if he has a tan and looks fit. Yet on Wall Street there would be serious suspicion if that man kept his tan more than a week past vacation.

California's climate is not only good for sports, it is also a recognized breeding ground for new ideas. Racquetball is both a new sport and a new idea—and prospers doubly as a result.

Why is climate important for a sport that is played indoors? Simply because it's easier to travel to an indoor club in warm weather. Rain, snow, and the cold discourage families from leaving their homes. In addition, training is easier in sunshine, which partially explains why San Diego is more conducive to racquetball than elsewhere in California: despite tourist proclamations to the contrary, an athlete can run year-round on beaches only as far south as Newport Beach and San Diego.

The San Diego setting merely provides the fertile surroundings for racquetball to grow. But in the first instance there had to be a healthy seed implanted that could ripen. There was, and that seed had two parts —a pioneer core of players and two of the sport's biggest equipment manufacturers, Ektelon and Leach Industries.

A cadre of top paddleball players already lived in San Diego when the crossover to racquetball started in 1969. Dr. Charles Hanna, Carl Loveday, Dr. Bud Muehleisen, and Charlie Brumfield were devotees of the game played with a solid—no strings—wooden paddle. In fact, Muehleisen won the national paddleball championships in 1966 and 1968—then his title was taken over by Brumfield in 1969 and 1970. The spiritual leader of the foursome was Carl Loveday, already a superstar in badminton who applied his skill in that sport to both paddleball and racquetball. He had a simple ABC of instruction for his disciples: The letters stood for Always Believe Carl.

When the group traveled to the early racquetball nationals, there was an unspoken *esprit de corps*, which took the form of rooting for fellow San Diegans. When Brumfield won his first racquetball nationals in 1972, the rest of the crew was there to watch. On an adjacent court that same year, Muehleisen won the masters (forty and over) singles, and the next year won the masters doubles with Loveday while Brumfield was repeating as national champion a few courts away.

When the Californians gathered to watch their lodge brothers in the different age divisions, the clique did not pass unnoticed. The San Diego spirit was beginning to fire up.

The first man to be drawn to San Diego partially because of its rabid racquetball reputation was Steve Keeley. Keeley studied veterinary medicine at Michigan State University and won the national paddleball title after playing the game just two years. Keeley quickly got bored with the all-wood paddle game and migrated to San Diego to pursue the veterinary profession. While waiting to take his medical boards, the fever of racquetball, with its excited talk of a pro tour, totally distracted him. He passed the exams six months later but abandoned the thought of practicing when it became clear he couldn't excel in racquetball simultaneously. In three years, Keeley became the second-biggest money-winner on the racquetball circuit.

The next racquetballer to migrate to San Diego was Steve Strandemo. But Strandemo was the *first* athlete to come to Southern California with the express purpose of becoming a racquetball superstar. He originally lived in St. Cloud, Minnesota, a small suburb of Minneapolis. Strandemo had played some pick-up racquetball locally, and in 1968 visited the historic national paddle-racquets championships in Minneapolis, where Midwesterners Bill Schmidke and Craig Finger were the sport's living legends.

Strandemo was so impressed and excited by what he saw that the next year he went to the first racquetball nationals in St. Louis, where he was thrashed in the first round by a player who in his next match lost both games to Brumfield by a score of 19–0.

"Jesus, Brum had him 19–0; I wondered what the hell he'd have me?" Strandemo mused with awe.

"But I wanted a crack at getting good. I wasn't learning any technique in Minnesota. I couldn't get close to winning against Finger and Schmidke, the guys who lived nearby. They had my pattern pegged better than I had their pattern pegged. Psychologically they developed permanent wins over me.

"I was at a point where my athletic ability had taken me as far as it could, and I needed form and hard practice outside Minnesota, because I was just playing those two guys and getting virtually nowhere. I looked around to see where the technique masters were coming from: San Diego. Steve Keeley had made the move and was already better. He had excellent form.

"Brumfield had great form. Muehleisen, good form. Paul Lawrence, a former paddleball champ and another transplant from Michigan to San Diego, good form.

"I knew I needed a lot of work just watching the other guy's technique and then developing a mirror swing myself. Jesus, I concentrated hard. Played night and day and ran on the beach in between. I played at Gorham's and never even had a car. I lived with a cousin and spent zero. I earned seventeen hundred dollars on the tour the first year and saved money."

After four years on the racquetball tour, Strandemo was a superstar and one of the game's top money-winners.

After Keeley and Strandemo, it was a traffic jam to San Diego. First, Steve Serrot, the wonder kid ripened from the St. Louis Jewish Community Center program, had a fabulous record as an eighteen-year-old, came West, and promptly fell back into the pro pack—but not before he put the finishing touches on the finest strokes in the game's young history in San Diego. Then eighteen-year-old Marty Hogan, the 1977 tour phenomenon, left St. Louis and set up residence in San Diego, where he goes to college and practices and perfects his racquetball nonstop.

Afterward it was St. Louis stars, Jerry Hilecher and Ben Kolton. Then Davey Bledsoe, came from Memphis, Richie Wagner from New Jersey, and even Steve Mondry, the promising amateur.

Strandemo described the zeal of Mondry: "He's a typical example of a racquetball freak. He's out here just playing racquetball and giving a few lessons to eat. He's not even involved with a sponsor. He doesn't want the distraction of working for a company while he's getting his game together. You can't do both until you've got your act together.

"Somewhere along the line Mondry's going to have to make a decision. The game will make the decision for him if his progress is solid. If he gets good, one of the companies will pick him up and put him on salary to give clinics. Otherwise it's tough to keep going giving lessons for ten dollars a pop."

Not everyone who comes to San Diego will make it as a superstar. There's not enough room. But that doesn't stop the traffic.

Strandemo pointed to Bill Burnett, a young kid from Vermont. "He's just come out from the East. I don't know if he's going to make it. Honestly, he's going to need lessons, and I don't know who's going to give him help. Unless you're really attentive, you can't pick it up by yourself. You need someone to convey the words of the action. If you've got the ability and some smarts and come out to San Diego, you can pick this game up. If not, forget it; the sport's too tough."

One player who came to San Diego and made it instantly was Shannon Wright, formerly of Dallas. Wright was the first woman to migrate to the mecca, though she was already ranked in the world's top four. But she zoomed to the absolute top by playing with San Diego's best men pros.

"Shannon's competent, aggressive, and has a very good backhand," Strandemo observed. "She got in with the guys, and her game improved immediately."

Despite San Diego's mystique as the heart of all racquetball, there are many other giant centers for the sport. Chicago, Denver, Atlanta, Hous-

ton, St. Louis, and Memphis all have such communities that rage over racquetball.

St. Louis, next to San Diego, is the most fanatic, largely because of the tremendous impact the local Jewish Community Center has had on racquetball. The JCC has spawned more of the sport's superstars than any other city in America: Marty Hogan, Steve Serrot, Jerry Hilecher, Ben Kolton, and Ken Wong are all products of the St. Louis JCC. But the lure of San Diego snatched the best ones away like a flame grabs the gaze of lovers to its center coals.

San Diego's allure fuels itself. More court clubs have been constructed in this city than anywhere else. Of the twenty-five facilities, George Brown's, Gorham's, and the Atlas Health Club are the most famous. The Atlas is a spiffy spa, with six lighted tennis courts, a jogging track, a twenty-five-meter pool, video tape systems, and exotic jacuzzi baths. It's so popular with its regular clientele that the stars often can't find a spot to practice in its crowded six-court schedule.

The Atlas club regularly hosts the national championship and is the perfect site with its controversial three glass walls suited for spectators and television.

Gorham's was the pro's first gathering place eight years ago. Everybody played at Gorham's. The group was closer knit than it is now, and the club's six courts were seemingly occupied all day by Strandemo, Brumfield, Keeley, Muehleisen, and Loveday. The sport wasn't professional then and the general public's interest wasn't that high, so the top pros could just drop in at noon or 9 P.M. and always find an open court.

Strandemo reminisced about those early years.

"We played punishment games at Gorham's. God, everybody was there. All that talent. It was unique. I remember getting into some mon-

strous exchanges with Brumfield. We'd sometimes rally for fifteen minutes in a single point and never kill the ball. Just pass it back and forth, back and forth. Three games to twenty-one like that was punishment."

The ritual changed because courts became busy with regular members and the club was inconvenient in downtown San Diego. Now virtually every ranking pro plays at George Brown's, on the city's northern perimeter.

Part of Brown's appeal is that it's close by to Leach Industries and Ektelon. And since all of racquetball's best professionals are employed by either Leach or Ektelon, it's like having courts in your backyard. It surely saves the commute downtown to Atlas in freeway traffic.

Brown's further attraction is that because athlete's schedules are not particularly disciplined, a player can zip across to the courts without having a game and likely pick up one with Brumfield, Hogan, Wagner, Serrot, Strandemo, Bledsoe, Keeley, Hilecher, Wright, or Mondry.

Brown's is not an elegant facility, and as you drive up it looks like an ordinary storefront, but inside more talent assembles than any other practice area in sport. The irony of this collection of solid-gold performers at Brown's is that the rest of the members don't even know who Charlie Brumfield or Marty Hogan are. In fact, one local came up to Brumfield while he was giving an interview in the corridor and asked him if he knew the rules.

"Who wins the point if the ball sails out of court?" he was asking the world's No. 1 player.

The fact that Brown's is uncrowded and is close to work is the main reason for its popularity among the pros, though the fact their employers pay for their membership has something to do with it.

Most analysis of why San Diego became racquetball's nerve center ends up in a chicken-or-the-egg dialogue—whether the players came to San Diego because it was the center or whether it became the center because players came West.

The single force that cuts through the question is the presence in San Diego of Leach Industries and Ektelon, the world's most prominent racquet manufacturers. Every leading player is under contract to either Leach or Ektelon to conduct clinics, assist in product development, recruit young players, and promote the company's product on tour.

Where tennis and golf professionals' identification with their sponsors is somewhat gentle—a modest initial W appearing on a Wilson shirt, a tiny crocodile on Izod products, or a penguin, golden bear, hang-ten feet on other apparel—Leach and Ektelon boldly print the company's name across the back and front of players' shirts.

Leach is aggressive in signing up the top pros and employs seven of the top ten men in the world. Three of those men—Hogan, Serrot, and Wagner—are being put through college by Leach at San Diego State University, so the lure of employer, sport, and university in the same city is compelling. Leach Industries required its three scholarship students to come to San Diego because the competition was better there than anywhere else.

Any movement needs the injection of personal energy to expand. Charlie Drake, an officer and owner of Leach, is one of the most influential men in racquetball, and certainly in San Diego he has the far-reaching power of a czar. He controls by contract the game's best players, and he decides to what extent Leach will sponsor the professional tour. Drake has made Leach a players' company by getting it involved in all phases of his pros' lives, including their education. He even created a subsidiary company owned totally by the Leach staff professionals for the purpose of promoting clinics and exhibitions around the country. Drake is an A-level racquetball player himself and is trusted by the pros as a result.

There is a theory that abounds in lofty racquetball circles that the game was prevented from developing in San Diego by one of the city's best players, Dr. Bud Muehleisen. The concept suggests, with an almost Freudian twist, that the doctor held a unique position in the sport and went all over the country as one of the "best" players, indeed, winning the nationals twice. He reportedly held Charlie Brumfield's progress back almost three years by phoning tournament directors who were personal friends and influencing the seeding of the draws. He'd say that he had this kid who's coming along, not doing really well, but who should get a chance to play some of the seeded players. In fact, Brumfield was beating the good doctor in practice. Brumfield would get slotted in the draw alongside Craig Finger and Paul Lawrence, two of the best players. Muehleisen, meanwhile, would sail to the finals in the other side of the draw without drawing a deep breath.

Charlie would beat both Finger and Lawrence in marathon matches and then have to play Muehleisen in the finals. And if that weren't enough, the doctor would switch the scheduling so that the doubles would be played before the singles finals. Brumfield's partner was his tormentor, Muehleisen, and their style of play dictated that while the doctor hung back, Charlie would do 90 per cent of the running. People asked Brumfield why he tolerated being finagled, and his response was that he was so busy going to college and law school, it was simpler to have Bud make all his travel and tournament plans.

Charlie Drake considers Brumfield to have been one of the country's best players in both paddleball and racquetball from 1962 on, though he didn't win the racquetball nationals till 1972. The reason? Drake thinks Muehleisen held both the game and Brumfield down for years. "Bud kept club development in San Diego in the Dark Ages," Drake concluded.

While one can list the elements of San Diego's racquetball mania, its overall mystique is an intangible. The fabulous court-club facilities, the weather, Leach Industries, and the superstars are all ingredients of the city's magnetism, yet the phenomenon now feeds on itself. The stars gravitate to San Diego because the stars are already there—and so on. It is not so important to trace why San Diego is the center of the racquetball tempest as to observe that it is so—and that it will continue. Ultimately the reality and the myths merge—and players are drawn to San Diego in much the same way as the religious fanatic follows the call to Mecca: In the end the prophecy fulfills itself.

Steve Strandemo summed up San Diego's spirit:

"You know, I always played a team sport before racquetball. Suddenly I was my own coach, general manager, and trainer. I quickly reached a plateau in the sport where my maximum potential was still miles away. I wanted to be drawn somewhere. I didn't give a damn where it was—New York, Florida, wherever the action was. San Diego had the reputation for guys running on the beach, singing songs, pounding their chests. I came out here the summer before the game went professional in 1973. There was no money, and still we played all day long. It was tough to get on top and tougher to stay on top. But it's not an impossible game. Hell, snap your wrist, run like hell, and you can't go far wrong."

One might suppose that if racquetball is truly a cult with a language and people all of its own, its teaching methods should be as fanatic as the enthusiasm that drives the sport. A space-age game should have space-age instruction.

It's true that conventional learning takes too long. The fact that it takes twelve years of basic schooling before we are prepared for college is a sign that our educational system is not streamlined. It also takes ten years of intensive training to become an accomplished athlete in any sport: golf, tennis, football, ice hockey. It shouldn't take so long, and one day it won't.

Soon it will become apparent that memorizing vocabulary words, Latin phrases, or famous dates in history is an absurd ritual—just as there must be a better way to learn golf than to hit ten thousand drives on a practice tee; a better way to learn tennis than to bash ten thousand practice serves; or a better way to hit a pinch forehand in racquetball than to drop and kill ten thousand shots in solo session.

The ultimate teaching technique must involve a more productive method for harnessing the powers of the mind. If we were to close our eyes and imagine the elements of such a futuristic learning process, they might include the critical ingredients of biofeedback, Zen, and Masters and Johnson.

In essence, biofeedback teaches that an individual has extraordinary control over his body—a discipline largely unexplored to date. It involves the normal buzz words associated with every sport—reflexes, anticipation, and intuition—words that are granted almost mystical meaning and, as a result, are assumed unable to be taught. In customary instruction manuals, it is taken for granted that only gifted athletes have good reflexes, anticipation, and intuition.

Biofeedback is a discipline that insists these qualities can be learned—not by conventional teaching methods and not necessarily oncourt. In essence, biofeedback shows that a man (an athlete) can control his biological and mental functioning through revelations of the mind's unconscious reactions to reality. This is in part accomplished through measuring the control of muscles, heartbeat, and brain waves, and even through meditation. And, of course, the methods are not singled out for application to racquetball alone. But because racquetball is such a new game and its techniques so primitive, the science of biofeedback is probably more immediately useful—even to help develop technique—than in tennis or golf, which have been played for over a century with reasonably sophisticated learning schemes.

There is a famous tome on Zen by Eugene Herigel, *Zen on Archery*, that has been, more or less, Westernized to make Chinese thinking acceptable to our palate. Steve Keeley, the twenty-eight-year-old veteran racquetball star and part of racquetball history himself, is imbued with the Zen spirit, though he uses the language of Tim Galwey's *Inner Game of Tennis* (Self I and Self II) to describe his mentality. Basically, the idea is to unclutter your mind from all extraneous thought. The pressures of trying to win this or that point, hating your opponent, or worrying about your equipment and court conditions are frozen out of the consciousness.

Even contemplating strategy or strokes is forbidden in ideal Zen practice. This concept doesn't mean that the mind is not involved in the learning process. It does mean that the process should be automatic—like a computer receiving data. For example, if you mishit a serve, you simply make the observation that the serve was mishit—not the judgment that you hit a horrible serve and are a horrible player.

The mind will then make the appropriate adjustment without going through the gyrations of telling yourself to make a grip change, open the racquet face, or rotate your shoulders. The mind operates faster than oral instructions—that is, if you keep it free of trivia—talking to yourself, feeding verbal input or self-criticism.

If the student watches the pros play or hits a thousand forehands against the front wall, each experience is cranked into the memory bank for later use. The problem, naturally, is to be able to recall this information instantaneously when it's needed oncourt. This involves keeping your mind a clean slate so that data retrieval is not blocked by bric-a-brac. In Zen, this is called a "beginner's mind." The trick is to keep your conscious head a beginner's mind, free of prejudice, emotions, and rational exercise.

Even if you accept biofeedback and Zen skeptically as vital disciplines in learning racquetball, you may have difficulty believing that Masters and Johnson have any relevance whatsoever to court sports. That's a shame, because an essential theme of the world's most heralded clinical psychologists is directly pertinent to racquetball.

Masters and Johnson's most publicized work has been in the area of sexual dysfunction, and if you don't think sexuality is a critical force in all athletics, just look around you.

All the adjectives describing a champion athlete—strong, powerful, fast, well-conditioned, and fit—are *macho* words with definite male identification. Even words like graceful, serene, and stylish—though genderless in nature—can enhance the overall reputation of any sportsman or sportswoman.

Athletes are continually conscious of their own sexuality, and their dress is part of that concern. For example, racquetball players will either roll down their socks or wear high calf-length socks, whichever improves the musculature of their leg line. And any racquet sport player is proud of his racquet arm—just as a weight lifter, football player, or even jockey is pleased with his physique. One of the Masters and Johnson techniques for resolving dysfunction is to remove the emphasis on performance. This concept can either be used to help a racquetball player out of a slump or to assist him reach a higher level of excellence.

It sounds like a paradox that to improve performance you cease thinking about it, but that's exactly what is meant. It's a method for improving your standard by not thinking about it—in other words, just hit the ball and not worry whether it is a kill or a rollout.

The brain already knows the standards for excellence, so you should concentrate on the harmony of striking the ball without getting into the problem of winning or losing.

Obviously, one cares about the end result of winning, but remember, we are only talking about the method for getting there. This involves eliminating the constant anxiety of a mind that says threateningly, "You must win the next point, you must win this point." For if you lose the point, your anxiety is doubled, repression solidifies, and you'll likely lose a lot more of the next points.

You must remember that biofeedback, Zen, and clinical psychology theory are disciplines that have a remarkable degree of similar elements. They are not to be adopted blindly without attending to stroke analysis or strategy. There must be a balance to succeed at any competitive level.

Racquetballers already seem to be aware of the predicament of getting the mind as fit as the body. Their language is filled with phrases referring to the problem. For example, Charlie Brumfield refers to those players who can't function because of overexamination of oncourt situations as being crippled by "paralysis via analysis." Steve Keeley has an even more vivid expression for those who seize up mentally in a match as being afflicted with "Blinkus of the Thinkus." Not exactly coinage that would qualify for the biofeedback lexicon, but racquetball promises a fast-learning curve, instant enjoyment, and no frills, remember?

The current "bulletball" phenomenon will not last. The manufacturers know it is not in the best interests of players, spectators, nor ultimately a television audience. But the ball companies have experimented widely with different rubber products and molding processes to develop a uniform effective ball. Their machines, formulas, and fabrication techniques will only be altered when the current raw material and ball stock run out. It is doubtful if any company will swallow an entire inventory to accommodate the need for a slightly slower ball.

Racquets have already improved in technology from wood to tubular steel to extruded aluminum to Fiberglas and currently to exotic composites of glass and metal and graphite. With each change, the velocity of the ball increases, thereby changing strokes to meet the new speed. A player will emphasize shooting more if he realizes he'll get a premium not only for the normal kill zone, but even for a reduced risk shot—one higher off the floor and easier to execute. A safe shot with a fast ball will pay better dividends (because of its added speed) than the high-risk shot with a dead ball.

As this stroke evolution become complete, all instruction and illustrations on control and steadiness become obsolete.

Rules changes affect technique also. For example, when the rules were altered to eliminate the third or final game, substituting the tiebreaks instead, a shooting style became even more mandatory. Control and steadiness were fine when the marathon match was played, on the theory that over a long period of time, percentage play favored consistency. This is analogous to challenging Jack Nicklaus to a million-dollar winner-take-all golf match. If you were selecting the conditions, you would pick a one-hole match (par three). If Nicklaus were choosing he'd want at least eighteen holes and probably thirty-six to maximize the percentages in his favor.

In other words, anyone can get lucky for a single shot—Nicklaus could shank and you could hit pin high. The tiebreak reduces the match to a game of chance.

When racquets, balls, rules, and courts finally standardize, instruction methods will also standardize. Thereafter, methods will undergo gradual modification, but from a base of common denominators such as similar ball speed, regulated racquet flex, and identical glass-court playing characteristics.

Stroke development will follow equipment changes in the next several years, although some of the technology may weave forward and backward, like the Lewis and Clark expedition looking for a path through the wilderness.

At the outset of the instruction material, it is critical to remember two teaching commandments applicable to many sports—but specifically suited to racquetball. First, there is no right or wrong way to grip a racquet or stroke a ball. There are broad guidelines within which personal choice should play an important role. Also, don't be afraid to experiment with your own personal choices. The obsession with finding the "right" grip is an exercise in rainbow chasing that detracts from the more important mission of practicing the shot most comfortable for you now. If the "now" mutates to something different, fine: Change the stroke slightly and get on with it.

The problem with seeking the perfect technique is that it doesn't exist. In addition, the search disrupts concentration with anxiety and frustration.

The second commandment is that the practice device of solo sessions smacking forehands and backhands in endless repetitions is the only sure way to improve. Unlike tennis, where you can't practice alone—except for the serve—or golf, where a driving range doesn't keep the ball in close enough contact to examine results precisely, racquetball solitaire can present exact match situations in terms of shooting for the low-wall kill or near kill. This is not done by rallying the ball to yourself against the front wall, but by setting up for a simple stroke against front wall, back wall, or sidewalls, and going for the shot. And then fetching the ball and doing it over again. And again. And again.

It's not easy, and it may be boring at times, but it is the only certifiable device for improvement. Charlie Brumfield, the world's No. 1, agonizes over the thought that if he wants to learn a new shot, it will take him two weeks on a court hitting ten thousand shots in cookie-cutter fashion.

A pro racquetball tour? Well, it hasn't reached the outrageous magnitude of the pro tennis or golf circuits, but the twelve-city Leach-Seamco 1977 tour is big-time professional sports—only in miniature.

Instead of having 400 world-ranked tennis players compete yearly for $8 million in prize money or 150 full-time touring golfers shoot for $10 million in purses, there are 18 ranked men and 12 women dividing up a lilliputian $100,000. The top men's prize each week is $2,000, while first place in the women's division is worth $740.

And though the total money offered for each round will double by the time this book is published, it is unlikely that the winnings of any racquetball player will soon compare with the absurd salaries taken home by pro basketball or football players. The reason for this is that the structure of pro racquetball was organized sensibly, with the companies that subsidize the sport controlling the players rather than vice versa.

Leach Industries, the major racquetball equipment manufacturer, hired the bulk of the leading players, including Charlie Brumfield, the world's No. 1; Marty Hogan, his apparent successor; Steve Keeley, one of the game's veterans at twenty-seven: Davey Bledsoe; Steve Serrot; Mike Zeitman; and Richard Wagner—in toto, seven out of ten of the best players in the nation.

Two of the remaining ten, Steve Strandemo and Jerry Hilecher, are under contract to Ektelon, another equipment maker. Because the prize money is so modest, none of the pros can truly make their living oncourt and must be subsidized. Depending on their ranking, each touring pro is paid a yearly salary by his equipment manufacturer for giving clinics at various court clubs around the country and for consulting on possible racquet designs and improvements. In addition, the company pays the pros' travel round trip to each tournament and picks up all his expenses as well. This means that the athlete can bank his prize winnings in total.

The system is sound, for it prevents the prize money from rocketing out of sight before there is sufficient spectator and television interest to warrant such escalation. And since the pros are hired by the companies putting up the prize money, it is unlikely they will complain about the paltry first-round losers' money—or the meager winner's check, for that matter.

It has been said that Leach Industries has a monopoly over racquetball by virtue of its having seven of the top ten pros on its staff, by underwriting the pro tour, and by being the leading equipment maker.

Surely Leach has many detractors in the game, just as any company that has the prime visibility in its market is going to be the prime target for criticism. And occasionally Leach has applied unfair pressure to maintain their image as the No. 1 force in racquetball, such as when Leach forced nonstaffer Steve Strandemo out of his clinic business in Steamboat Springs, Colorado, by offering his resort a better deal than maverick Strandemo could afford.

But the flip side of the coin is that without Leach none of the pros would have a profession in the sport, including Steve Strandemo. And to date, Leach has been fair in the overall racquetball business, whereas if it had a really ruthless streak, it could have undercut all the other manu-

facturers in price and driven them out of the marketplace. One assumes that their temperance is not simply the product of antitrust prohibitions against such unfair tactics. After all, there seems to be enough growth to go around, as virtually every racquet maker is back-ordered by six months and currently can't keep pace with the demand for equipment.

Seamco Sporting Goods Company is a joint sponsor of the tour, providing the "official" ball (Leach is the "official" racquet) for all tournaments. Perhaps because Seamco does not have any players under contract, its role has less impact than Leach's.

It is still too early in the game's genesis to consider what impact Leach and Seamco will have on the continuing progress of racquetball. In other sports, major companies have popped in looking for exposure at the ground-floor level and planning to ride the boom to its crest for maximum exposure. The roll call of companies dropping out of tournament sponsorship is lengthy indeed. But in the instance of golf or tennis, where the companies were not given or did not take a stake in the game at an early stage, the opportunity didn't exist to participate in the long term without twenty other companies being able to dilute their exposure by putting up more money more often.

One thing is certain. Leach and Seamco managements were bold when there was no assurance that racquetball would be a wildly popular sport. There was an element of risk involved. After all, racquetball's physical components are not that exciting: Four stark white walls, no net, no targets, not even a telltale do not exactly explode the imagination.

But sponsors in other minor sports often were only willing to test the water with their little toes, and even if the water was found to be alluring, by the time the test was over, dozens of other companies were knocking aside the first in.

Leach Industries, at least, will not be pushed aside so easily, as it has fully integrated its involvement vertically, through player contracts, equipment manufacturing, and tour sponsorship.

The tour itself is a fascinating cross section of the game's most exciting as well as its most prosaic components. More than any other sport, the racquetball hacker can identify with the professional circuit. It's not easy to discern why, either. The spread in talent between a club player and a touring pro is far greater than in tennis or golf. Charlie Brumfield would not lose a point to a B player, yet Jimmy Connors might lose a half dozen or so points in a set to a B ladder tennis player.

Maybe the closeness of the pro game to the club game is because the stars are still in touch with reality without million-dollar contracts to flip them out into an obnoxious fantasy world. Charlie Brumfield is not reluctant to settle his hulking frame on a clubhouse sofa and preach racquetball lore to anyone who will listen. One can hardly imagine Arthur Ashe or Jack Nicklaus having the time to indulge clubbers in similar fashion. It's too bad racquetball isn't bigger because, Brumfield on the hustings is a far better act than either Nicklaus or Ashe. Take it from one who has listened to all three.

The nature of racquetball has something to do with the proximity of the pros to the fans. Tennis and golf were the exclusive property of the idle and the rich until ten years ago. Both were played solely in fancy aristocratic clubs—hardly the setting for a few beers between the superstars and spectators. Baseball, basketball, and football, while appealing to the appetite of the masses, has a different problem: The fans are separated from the players by a concrete stadium, and mingling with the crowd is not only not encouraged, it is forbidden. Fields are policed by cordons of grim-looking guards.

Racquetball, on the other hand, with its YMCA, YWCA, public court-club setting, greets all comers heartily. And that spirit shows.

I have chosen one of the stops on the 1976–77 Leach-Seamco tour as a narrative device to exhibit the character of competitive racquetball. The site selected in Fort Lauderdale was not the biggest on the tour, nor the most glamorous, nor was it the smallest or the most provincial. It did, however, amplify the sport's heartbeat fairly without exaggeration, yet with no false modesty, either.

The name of the event was the Court Rooms Pro/Am, December 2–5, 1976, which is not exactly a title to ignite the spleen of sports lovers everywhere. The Court Rooms is a handsome racquetball and health club in North Fort Lauderdale, with seven regulation four-wall courts all with glass back walls plus a seven-foot Advent television screen with closed-circuit capabilities on every court.

The facility was big-league; the title was not. Everyone associates Pro/Am with either the golf "hit and giggle" before the main tournament or the "poke and run" tennis events that have been shunned by television for years because of their bush-league entertainment value. In fact, all the titles on the racquetball tour should be dressed up to sound meaningful. It's so simple. The Florida stop could be called the Southern Championships, the Vermont event changed to the Eastern Championships; the Houston tournament switched to the North American Open; and somewhere, the World Championships.

But with so little history behind organized racquetball, labels of pro tour events are low-priority, while in dozens of other areas slick innovations of sister sports have been copied instantly, and in some cases new ideas have actually been developed independently. The latter case best projects the sport's excitement.

One of the bizarre features of an emerging pro sport is that there is utterly free access to competition. There is no tournament bureau, as in golf, where pros must pass a written and playing test that by its nature limits those accepted on tour to a select few. In tennis, entry to tournaments is controlled by a computer ranking system that lists 400 competitors, which is somewhat redundant in that the largest tournaments in the world—Wimbledon, Flushing Meadows, and the French Championship —only can accommodate 128 players, and most events have fields of 32.

But though there are 3 million racquetball players, apparently not many know how easy it is to enter a pro tournament. No ranking, no skill, and not even a racquet are required (you can borrow one) to sign up for a major tour championship. I know. Having never been inside a racquetball court before, I fired off an application to the Court Rooms Pro/Am together with my check for twenty-five dollars. (I hadn't the foggiest idea whether my application would be accepted, but I didn't want to be rejected on a procedural omission.)

The application itself had no blank space to include one's record, so I didn't understand how the committee would determine my caliber of play from my address, phone number, and T-shirt size which were all the pertinent data required on the entry form clipped from the September issue of *National Racquetball* magazine.

I never heard a peep from the Court Rooms as to whether my entry had been accepted, and frankly it would be *gauche* of me to call and ask. After all, it was their world—not mine—and if the procedure was to assume everybody ought to know their status without being told, who was I to rock the boat by asking?

I was going to Fort Lauderdale anyway to examine the tour first hand for the book, so I could afford to be as cool as they.

My plane landed in Fort Lauderdale at noon the day the tournament was scheduled to begin. I walked into the club an hour later and immediately scanned the draw sheet as casually as possible so no one would notice my chagrin if my name was not listed. But there it was: I was posted to play an hour later against a chap called Skip from Illinois. Hmmmmmm. A long way to come if this guy is a beginner like me. I had hoped to draw a local under the assumption that some old geezer might be used to fill in vacant spots in the field. I later learned that even the old geezers would have stomped me.

Maybe Skip would have the same worry when he saw my name from New York City, the home of the New York Knicks, Jets, Giants, Apples, and many other tough people. I hastily checked in, trying to be as non-chalant as possible, a façade that was crushed by my asking how many games one played in the first round.

Can you imagine the scene? It was as if I had entered the U. S. Open Golf tournament and my entry had been accepted along with Jack Nicklaus, Arnold Palmer, and Johnny Miller without my ever having played a single round of golf!!! Or being accepted at Wimbledon without knowing the difference between a let and an ace!!!

I gave myself away with every breath. After collecting my free Leach-Seamco T-shirt given all competitors—a smart move because none of the pros have clothes contracts, and the freebies with sponsors' names blazing across the back are worn by even the veteran pros with the enthusiasm of an adolescent camper wearing his troop's colors for the first time—I retreated to the locker room to change for my match.

The was the first of many false starts. I looked at the small metal cubicle and quickly deduced that my suit would have to be rolled into a ball to fit, but racquetball is, after all, the sport for the masses, and I was the only chap in the neighborhood wearing a jacket. I would adjust.

My tape recorder was another matter. Purchased for $29.95 the night before to record permanently the noises of racquetballers, like a bird watcher might want to preserve the ornate sounds of the spotted mud warbler, it would fit into the locker, but there was no lock. (They don't wear jackets in Fort Lauderdale, but does that mean they don't pilfer?)

I returned sheepishly upstairs to the front desk and asked for a lock.

I changed quickly—my match was ten minutes away—before noticing that my sneakers had last been used for tennis on clay, which meant that what appeared to be twenty pounds of the court's gritty surface had lodged in the treads of each sole. My God!! I would leave a trail of brown footprints all over the white floor and be in disgrace. I felt like the duck hunter who comes home with boots caked with mud and takes only the first step into the hallway tufted carpet before retreating outdoors in shame.

But I couldn't go outdoors. I would be blackballed by the racquetball organization and never be allowed to fetch material for the book. I took off the shoes and shook them fiercely—onto the new locker-room rug, fortunately colored a dark green hue, which would camouflage my tracks for a few minutes. I finished the job whacking the soles against a large wastebasket, which by virtue of my contribution was converted into a giant flowerpot—without flowers but with plenty of soil.

Only two more minor accidents came between me and my first visit to a racquetball court—forgetting a towel, which required another shameful trip to the front desk, and putting the combination lock on backward, which meant that after my match I would have to stand on my head to twirl the numbers. The latter accident is easily explainable in terms of my own crusty club background, where lockers did not have locks of any sort. I simply did not understand that a combination lock had a front and a back. The myth that members of the Piping Rock Club or River Club steal less than those at YMCAs or public court clubs is perpetuated by the members of the establishment organizations themselves.

I appeared at the glass doors of an assigned court, where my opponent was already crashing forehands and backhands mightily against the front wall. Upon seeing me, he hastily came outside, as if my spying on his practice session was unsporting.

Skip introduced himself and said he was through and I could have the court to myself. This was my introduction to the custom in racquetball of not practicing with your opponent beforehand. You do it alone.

Come to think of it, this makes sense. Why would you go out for a friendly knock-up with a man who in a few seconds time will be at your throat—or at least around your shoulders and snapping your heels? It would be like the football Giants scrimmaging against the Jets for a few moments before kickoff. Or Bobby Hull firing practice shots against an opposing goalie in the warm-up. If tennis had any wits, it would eliminate the warm-up altogether as a waste of time and bush-league drama. Wouldn't it be far more exciting, for example, to have Jimmy Connors and Bjorn Borg simply walk on center court and begin to play straightaway? No practice rallies, no volleys, just right up to the baseline and serve.

Another lesson that might be learned from racquetball tournaments is that the players act as referees in the early rounds. Jean Souser, one of the leading players on the women's tour, appeared at the top of the back glass wall, threw a green ball down into the pit, and asked politely, "Players ready?"

There are no rough or smooth strings on a racquetball racket, so the referee drops a coin from the gallery. I lost the toss but smacked my opponent's first serve two inches above the front wall floor for a near rollout, winning the right to serve. It was the closest I came to being a player that afternoon.

I pushed up a lame serve into the corner—not knowing how to deliver a Z or reverse Garfinkle—and watched my foe beat the ball front wall, sidewall so that I could only turn around and marvel at its speed and accuracy.

Skip quickly moved to 5–0, though I had sided him out twice, but now I feared I might be bagled (21–0). Just as anxiety was turning into brooding, my man missed a sitter and I cruised a low pass beyond his left side: 7–1. My points did not exactly come in bunches after that, but I did manage to reach 21–6. I was not even winded, and with good reason. I couldn't stay in the rallies long enough to keep warm, and I was amazed when we were given a five-minute rest period after the first game.

Skip was leading in the second game, 7–3, when he called a time-out. I thought he was joking, but the referee informed me both of us were entitled to three one-minute time-outs per game. The match was quickly over 21–6, 21–8, and I retreated to the locker room to fiddle with my upside-down combination lock.

Fifteen minutes later, I reviewed my match and was perplexed why I was so intimidated. I was sure I could do better next time, but there were no consolation singles, and the courts were booked solidly with matches for the rest of the weekend. My opponent asked me why I hadn't entered the amateur singles, which was being run simultaneously with the pro event. He reported a procedure that must be unique to racquetball: A player may play in amateur events until he has won $500 in a season. Five hundred dollars is not a lot of loot but, quarter-finalists only get $250, so you have to be an accomplished pro to win $500 in a year. Outsiders rarely crack the top ten through upsets.

While this ersatz amateur role might offend purists, it is fair to encourage participation at all levels, and it also provides an excellent farm system for the pros. For example, Steve Mondry, the top amateur in 1977, played in both the pro event, where he lost in the second round, and in the amateur, which he won, thereby giving him an incredible amount of match experience in a week.

The governing fathers of racquetball even think of the novice spectators as well. If you were to walk into the Court Rooms and see seven matches being run simultaneously, you would not immediately know who were the pros and who the amateurs—except that the tour rules provide that a black Seamco ball will be used for amateur events and a green one for pro matches.

As I packed my bag, a thousand impressions tickled my awareness, the first being that a pro racquetballer can tuck his rackets in a suitcase and no one would ever know he was a professional athlete. Unlike tennis, where the pro exults in tucking six rackets under his arm in a airport. There is no doubt about it: He is a pro tennis player. No tennis pro would think of hiding his pile of Wilsons or Dunlops in a suitcase.

There is a congenial informality about a pro racquetball tournament that has long since fled from the tennis and golf scenes. Cold cuts, fruit, salad, and Gatorade are left on a table in a hospitality area for players. None of the players wears a sport jacket in the clubhouse. Indeed, none of the spectators do, either. In the men's room stalls there are no coat hooks whatsoever.

Scheduling is still slipshod in the racquetball pro ranks, where two matches scheduled in a day are not unusual, and even in the later rounds a seeded player might finish a quarter-final at 11 P.M. and have to be on-court the next morning at ten.

The most exciting element about the racquetball tour is that there are no precedents holding back innovation. If the Association feels a change will be good for the sport, the change is effected immediately. No waiting around for annual meetings, board gatherings, or special rules sessions.

This atmosphere of experimentation and open-mindedness is displayed across the board—in the language of the sport, in player behavior, and in style of play.

Charlie Brumfield, the Babe Ruth of racquetball, took my tape recorder during the finals of the Court Rooms Pro/Am between Marty
Hogan, the tour leader and everybody's pick to succeed Charlie as the
world's No. 1, and Davey Bledsoe, a twenty-five-year-old relative newcomer who is a gifted athlete, with a graceful style and a high-strung dis-
position. Bledsoe won the first game over Hogan in a stunning reversal of
form. Hogan steadied somewhat in the second game and ran to a modest
15–8 lead when Brumfield pushed the recorder button for the first time.

"Hogan has an execution ratio superiority now and scores on a reverse
pinch forehand: 17–9.

"Bledsoe is wasting his resources for the tiebreak. Sideout. Hogan still
not playing with intensity. Davey, way behind in second game, races
from sidewall to sidewall and is wasting his adrenalin flush.

"Hogan scores right wall, front wall: 18–11." [Suddenly the silence is
broken by a guttural wild animal shout, "Shoot it, Hogan!!" The noise
has come from Hogan himself. Since there is no tradition for silence either in the gallery or from the players, as in tennis, dialogue between
players in racquetball—though at first disquieting—is quickly accepted as
part of the sport's culture. The bellowing back and forth adds both color
and excitement. The message is never profound, but when cried at
tackhammer level, its impact is startling. Already there is a move by
officials to stifle those who so assail the sport's decorum.]

"Bledsoe comes back with a drive down the line. Sideout and Marty is
agitated.

"[Now Bledsoe shrieks, 'Come on, generate!!'] Bledsoe should call a
time-out. He doesn't and gives Hogan time to drive. Good night, 19–12.
Hogan's arsenal is impressive, and he's hitting 5 per cent harder than at
the beginning of the match, but he's still sluggish.

"Bledsoe scores right wall, front wall. Mental error by Bledsoe. Game
Hogan, 21–14. Ten-minute rest before the tiebreak starts.

"Hogan rips the ball in the first point of the tiebreak. Bledsoe should
slow him down. Fluke ball. Sideout.

"['Break!!' Bledsoe sings at soprano level to acknowledge his luck.] It
is critical that he wins points early to make Hogan more cautious in shot
selection. Bledsoe should gamble. But he can't serve the ball off the back
wall to Hogan in tiebreak situation.

"Oh, oh! Hogan hits a photon. But the ball skipped and the ref didn't
call it. Bledsoe appeals and fortunately the linesman overheard me and
now calls the skip correctly.

"Whoop. A setup for Hogan—a gift from the Hanukkah God—but he
half misses it—appeal by Bledsoe. There's mass confusion in the gallery.
After polling the spectators, the point is decided for Hogan [laughter]:
1–1.

"Left-side crack attempt by Hogan. Bledsoe is making an error in
judgment by not slowing Hogan down: 3–2. Davey's shot selection is
suspect. Hogan could now gamble and blow this match open.

"Davey has lost his composure. He has two time-outs in the tiebreak
and should use one right now. Hogan puts up an all-time pumpkin.
Sideout. Fault. Davey's second serve should be put on waivers [laugh-
ter]. Sideout.

Davey Bledsoe in action against
Marty Hogan.

"Hogan squeezes ball. He firing up. 'Now I'm going to put it to you,'
Hogan yells. Second serve dies: 4–2. Bledsoe's coverage zone incorrect.
He dropped back too far, and Hogan's mishit went for a winner.
Official's time-out to wipe up the court. Fortunately, officials are doing
Bledsoe's job for him and slowing Hogan down.

"Davey has to learn more about controlling pace of play against an
adrenalin-style player like Hogan.

"Hogan serves, and Bledsoe shoots a hard drive to the left side. Hogan
returns well, with a wide-angle V. Bledsoe makes great get but ball
bounces weakly off back wall. Good night. A perfect drive down the
right side. That was the hardest ball of the tournament: 5–2. Danger
time for Davey. Two points could be all Bledsoe gets if Marty starts ex-
ploding. Marty appeals an obvious short serve. Upheld. He smiles. Lob

serve off back wall. Bledsoe returns and Hogan hits a BB: 6–2. Hogan misses. Sideout. 'Get the serve back,' Hogan calls.

" 'Keep it,' Bledsoe counters at the top of his lungs. Bledsoe misses and must call a time-out to slow Hogan down. He does. Thirty seconds to stop Hogan's momentum. Ace: 7–2.

"Davey down the right side but Hogan, on top of the ball, drills to the left. Skip ball: 9–2. This match is over. Another skip ball: 10–2. Match point. Bledsoe takes his second time-out. Hogan now will win his third straight NRC title. He's played excellent ball. He rarely hits the ball on the ground. And his shot moves with tremendous pace.

"Bledsoe drills uncharacteristic front wall and sidewall. Sideout. The golden retriever finally gets moving. He's psyching up. But it would have to be near Christmas for him to win this tiebreaker. Right-wall, front-wall winner: 4–10. Hogan screams, 'Don't miss those shots—quit playing around!!' Hogan coasting in normal style.

"Hinder call. Good judgment by Leve [Chuck Leve is the referee] on the shadow call. He's trying to redeem himself on two questionable decisions earlier in the tiebreaker.

"Bledsoe panics and tries to retrieve. Good night, Davey. You can't redrive the ball against Hogan, who never moves up for the kill-shot zone coverage. Match point. [Unlike tennis, this critical point is actually called as match point without worry that to do so is untraditional or *gauche*. Everyone knows it's match point in tennis, but the umpire imposes an artificial silence by calling the point as if it were like any other.]

"Hogan will probably try wide-angle crack serve. He does. But Bledsoe makes great return, forcing Hogan on defensive. Bledsoe panics again and flails from ten feet. Tiebreak and match to Hogan. Bledsoe's shot selection did him in during tiebreak."

Though the match was over, one cannot turn Brumfield off as easily as the tape machine. He talked of the old days when the racquetball style was more control—more meticulous strokemaking. But Charlie Brumfield is not a man to brood over the past. "The hot ball is better for TV," he affirmed. Still, he is not happy over many of the changes. The nationals, for instance, will be played on a court with three glass walls all the way to the floor. The kids like Hogan and Hilcher, who shoot rockets from the hip, will dominate, and the thinkers, the planners, the Renaissance racquetballers like Brum will struggle.

Another Renaissance man is Steve Keeley, twenty-seven years old and a doctor of veterinary medicine, though he has never practiced his profession and is not called "doctor" on tour. It is unlikely he ever will be unless it is in friendly acknowledgment of his being the essential core of the tour. He is popular—there's a word I haven't heard since college—with both the men and the women on the circuit. The younger players look to him for advice on travel plans, hotels, restaurants in the neighborhood, and general chitchat.

Keeley is the unofficial spokesman for the pros, though Brumfield doesn't respect him because he's not introspective enough about himself or the game. Basically Keeley is not smart enough for Brum, though this may be an unfair judgment in that Brum, a *magna cum laude* graduate from San Diego State, has exceptional intellectual dimension—without being boring or pedantic—and may be one of the brightest men in sports.

Others criticize Keeley from time to time because of his wandering spirit; some question whether is good for racquetball. For example, Keeley played his first-round opponent in Fort Lauderdale left-handed. To me this wasn't a display of arrogance, simply a gimmick to keep up his interest, which has waned noticeably in the past year. Steve Keeley is an angular man with no perceptible skills as an athlete other than his versatility. Even the simple shots he performs with a certain awkwardness. There was a time when Keeley practiced seven hours a day. But not now. He barely seems to have enough energy for his matches, and this lack of motivation crumbled him in Florida. He lost to one of the fresh young men on tour.

Steve Keeley.

If Keeley has lost his enthusiasm for playing the pro tour, he is redirecting his role as the chief anthologist for racquetball. He has written the sport's leading instruction book, is writing another, and has a cartoon and anecdote book in the works.

One of the colorful things about racquetball is its language. Keeley is the source of some of that language like "freak ball" or "bumblebee ball" or "psych factor," which he calls Keeleyisms, but more importantly, he records the phrases of others, particularly Brumfield. Charlie's brain has possibly been responsible for most of the argot of racquetball, as he mixes metaphors from other disciplines like psychology or business and applies them to his sport. Thus "adrenalin flush" has become a recognizable part of every racquetball player's makeup, though before Brumfield said it, no such flush apparently existed.

Keeley may be creating a far greater role for himself as historian and ultimately as the modern father of racquetball than Brumfield, whose playing records are untouchable and whose intellectual options may deter his ability to focus his talents on one life pursuit. Keeley seems to have already adjusted to his atrophied desire to play the tour and will concentrate instead on his writing, which from an untutored base shows a remarkable instinct for reporting the ordinary in clear sentences and energetic style.

One of the sport's stylish men is Steve Strandemo, twenty-six, who gave up his life as a schoolteacher in the Midwest at twenty-two to become a pro racquetballer. Because he did not learn the sport as a youngster, he had to find a way to accelerate to the top quickly. His method was to push himself into superhuman condition by training for seven to eight hours a day on the theory, "If your opponent can't breathe the last few points, you'll beat him."

Strandemo played the control game, had no big shots, yet ran the legs off younger and older foes alike. Then the ball became faster, and Steve

Steve Strandemo.

was forced to become a shooter and to learn to "float out" to the sides from center court. He is still in superb shape and wins matches combining wits with competitive guttiness. The signal of his style of play is colored on the back of both legs, where large round welts are patterned like an abstract line drawing. Most players have these telltale marks of their profession showing where the back of their thigh has gotten in the way of a killer forehand rocketing to the front wall.

It is an unusual ritual where no apologies are offered nor expected for a streak of lightning that smacks into your backside and flattens out like a dumdum bullet. The hit leaves a mark the size of a orange that turns colors from red to blue to a yellow-greenish hue. Apparently the idea is that if you get hit, you were in the way, and an "unavoidable hinder" is called, meaning the point is replayed—like a let in squash or tennis.

Strandemo explained that early in the week of a tournament he will stay in bed virtually all day to get rest, getting up only to eat or to practice. He knows that on Friday or Saturday night before a big match he won't be able to sleep much, so the nonstop napping beforehand will be invaluable.

Steve describes his first few rounds: "It looks as if I'll play Keeley or Kolton in the quarters, and it might not be pretty getting there. I need a challenge or my mind wanders. I'm afraid I'll lose interest so I'll have to be gutty to get to the later rounds."

He talks of the men on the tour. "Mondry? He's a gutty ass. He'll break into the top eight soon. He's a shotmaker with a good serve who plays crash.

"Mondry's got average speed and an average backhand but who's smart enough to go to the ceiling every time the ball comes in that direction. You know he's only twenty but he looks forty.

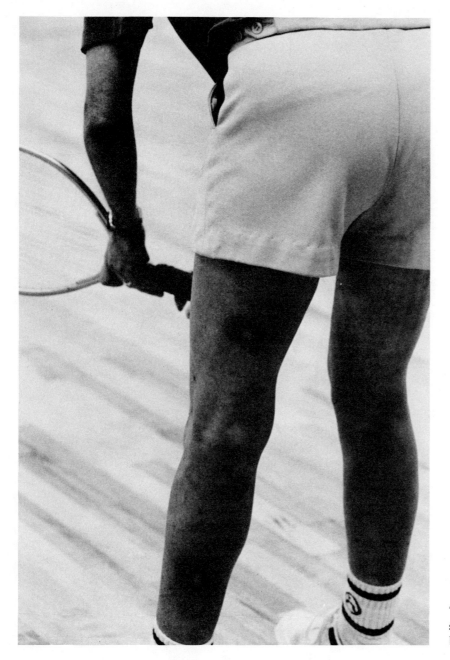

The backs of Peggy Steding's legs show the punishment racquetballers take from each other.

"Charlie Brumfield? Good timing, good muscle. You look at him in the shower and you'd think someone put two different people together. His upper and lower body.

"Vic Niederhoffer? [One of the world's best squash players who played three events on the racquetball tour in 1976.] Vic went as far as he could. He beat Hogan in Las Vegas and lost in the sixteens to Zeitman and then got to the quarters in St. Louis, where he was blown out by Steve Serrot. Those are damm good results reaching the top sixteen people in a sport with no preparation. He won a few times against people

Charlie Brumfield is a fierce competitor.

with thirty times the ability, but he always got the maximum out of his game. Heck, he didn't look like he could walk in a straight line.

"But Vic was never embarrassed in racquetball. He's too smart. He's that rare breed of athlete who knows when he should get out—and I respect him for it."

Jerry Hilecher, twenty-two, St. Louis, is a young pro who like Strandemo has style. His streaking serve and buggywhip rollouts enabled him to upset Brumfield and Hogan in Sacramento, where the front wall was all glass. Hilecher talked of friendship on the tour.

"People are friendly but maybe only to be polite. A lot of it is fake. A few years ago before the money, everyone seemed genuine in friendships. The money changed all that. I remember playing my best friend, Davey Bledsoe, a while back. We were very close. The match was mean and there was a lot of arguing, and the relationship was never the same afterward.

"The tour is too small. You're on the same side of the court with your opponent—talking to him—constantly next to him.

"When the game was strictly amateur, everyone seemed to be more friendly. That's changed and I'm more friendly to lesser players on tour —like Steve Mondry. Maybe when he cracks the top sixteen, the friendship will lessen. But I like Marty [Hogan the top money-winner] a lot. He's the Ilie Nastase of racquetball."

The one thing no one talked much about even when prodded was the natural factor of intimidation oncourt. There are not many sports where two antagonists go into combat right next to each other. Boxing and wrestling are examples, but combat is part of—not ancillary to—the game. In squash, there is two hundred years of genteel history brainwashing its players that only gentlemen play the game and if you crowd your honored foe, it is an accident. And you apologize immediately afterward.

In tennis there is a net separating rivals, so the issue of contact does not arise. But in racquetball there is no tradition and there is no net separating combatants, and as long as nothing more than a pewter spoon was at stake, the amateur ethic of a firm handshake between winner and loser would prevail. But inject a big bucket of bucks into a pro tour and the façade of gentility may vanish. It's too early to tell yet. The pro tour is still an infant without lawyers, agents, television, contracts, and fat endorsements. Whether a ghetto athlete faced with a 10-all situation and match point in the tiebreak for a $50,000 purse would fire a kill at the ankles of his adversary just to loosen him up is speculative but not unimaginable.

There are already signs that the competitors who crowd in racquetball have an edge. And depending how much you encroach on your opponent's shot sight line, you limit his options. For instance, if your tormentor is setting up behind you in the forehand corner, the closer you move to him, the more you restrict his stroke down the line. Flying elbows and brushing bodies are accidental but still more commonplace than five years ago. The intensity and potential violence of the pro tour, with two assailants attacking the ball—and maybe each other—if the frenzy follows its natural course is inestimable.

In football and ice hockey, where intimidation and brutality are inherent to the sport, referees and teammates close by act as deterrents and policemen to controlled warfare. For racquetball, with speed and power churning at close quarters, high-velocity tempers may be as natural a progression as the high-velocity ball. The racquetball pro tour, like the sport itself, is in a molten phase of becoming. Where the white-hot ichor of the game's superstars will ultimately flow is still being fought for.

A photo essay of the Charlie
Brumfield-Marty Hogan rivalry.

Official Racquetball Rules of the United States Racquetball Association (USRA) and National Racquetball Club (NRC)

The International Racquetball Association (IRA) is a rival organization to the USRA and the NRC and has its own official rules, which fortunately are almost identical in every area. The IRA's minor discrepencies are indicated by brackets.

Four-wall Rules

Rule 1.1 *Types of Games.* Racquetball may be played by two or four players. When played by two it is called "singles," and when played by four, "doubles."

Rule 1.2 *Description.* Racquetball, as the name implies, is a competitive game in which a racquet is used to serve and return the ball.

Rule 1.3 *Objective.* The objective is to win each volley [rally] by serving or returning the ball so the opponent is unable to keep the ball in play. A serve or volley [rally] is won when a side is unable to return the ball before it touches the floor twice.

RULE 1.4 *Points and Outs.* Points are scored only by the serving side when it serves an ace or wins a volley [rally]. When the serving side loses a volley it loses the serve. Losing the serve is call a "handout."

Rule 1.5 *Game.* A game is won by the side first scoring 21 points.

Rule 1.6 *Match.* A match is won by the side first winning 2 games.

Rule 1.7 *Tiebreak.*

Rule 2.1 *Court.* The specifications for the standard four-wall racquetball court are:

    a. *Dimension.* The dimensions shall be 20 feet wide, 20 feet high, and 40 feet long, with back wall at least 12 feet high.

    b. *Lines and Zones.* Racquetball courts shall be divided and marked on the floors with 1½-inch-wide red or white lines as follows:

        (1) *Short Line.* The short line is midway between and is parallel with the front and back walls dividing the court into equal front and back courts.

        (2) *Service Line.* The service line is parallel with and located 5 feet in front of the short line.

        (3) *Service Zone.* The service zone is the space between the outer edges of the short and service lines.

        (4) *Service Boxes.* A service box is located at each end of the service zone by lines 18 inches from and parallel with each sidewall.

        (5) *Receiving Lines.* Five feet back of the short line, vertical lines shall be marked on each sidewall extending 3 inches from the floor. See Rule 4.7(a).

Rule 2.2 *Ball Specifications*. The specifications for the standard racquetball are:

    a. *Official Ball*. The official ball of the USRA is the black Seamco 558; the official ball of the NRC is the green Seamco 559; [the IRA's official ball is the Seamco 444] or any other racquetball deemed official by the USRA or NRC from time to time. The ball shall be 2¼ inches in diameter; weight, approximately 1.40 ounces, with the bounce at 68–72 inches from 100-inch drop at a temperature of 76 degrees F.

Rule 2.3 *Ball Selection*. A new ball shall be selected by the referee for use in each match in all tournaments. During a game the referee may, at his discretion or at the request of both players or teams, select another ball. Balls that are not round or that bounce erratically shall not be used.

Rule 2.4 *Racquet*. The official racquet will have a maximum head length of 11 inches and a width of 9 inches. These measurements are computed from the outer edge of the racquet head rims. The handle may not exceed 7 inches in length. Total length and width of the racquet may not exceed a total of 27 inches.

    a. The racquet must include a thong, which must be securely wrapped on the player's wrist.

    b. The racquet frame may be made of any material, as long as it conforms to the above specifications.

    c. The strings of the racquet may be gut, monofilament, nylon, or metal.

Rule 2.5 *Uniform*. All parts of the uniform, consisting of shirt, shorts, and socks, shall be clean, white, or of bright colors. Warm-up pants and shirts, if worn in actual match play, shall also be white or of bright colors, but may be of any color if not used in match play. Only club insignia, name of club, name of racquetball organization, name of tournament, or name of sponsor may be on the uniform. Players may not play without shirts.

PART III. OFFICIATING

Rule 3.1 *Tournaments*. All tournaments shall be managed by a committee or chairman, who shall designate the officials.

Rule 3.2 *Officials*. The officials shall include a referee and a scorer. Additional assistants and record keepers may be designated as desired.

Rule 3.3 *Qualifications*. Since the quality of the officiating often determines the success of each tournament, all officials shall be experienced or trained, and shall be thoroughly familiar with these rules and with the local playing conditions.

Rule 3.4 *Rule Briefing*. Before all tournaments, all officials and players shall be briefed on rules and on local court hinders or other regulations.

Rule 3.5 *Referees.*

a. *Prematch Duties.* Before each match commences, it shall be the duty of the referee to:

(*1*) Check on adequacy of preparation of the court with respect to cleanliness, lighting, and temperature, and upon location of locker rooms, drinking fountains, etc.

(*2*) Check on availability and suitability of all materials necessary for the match, such as balls, towels, scorecards, and pencils.

(*3*) Check readiness and qualifications of assisting officials.

(*4*) Explain court regulations to players and inspect the compliance of racquets with rules.

(*5*) Remind players to have an adequate supply of extra racquets and uniforms.

(*6*) Introduce players, toss coin, and signal start of first game.

b. *Decisions.* During games the referee shall decide all questions that may arise in accordance with these rules. If there is body contact on the backswing, the player should call it quickly. This is the only call a player may make. On all questions involving judgment and on all questions not covered by these rules, the decision of the referee is final.

c. *Protests.* Any decision not involving the judgment of the referee may on protest be decided by the chairman, if present, or his delegated representative.

d. *Forfeitures.* A match may be forfeited by the referee when:

(*1*) Any player refuses to abide by the referee's decision, or engages in unsportsmanlike conduct.

(*2*) After warning, any player leaves the court without permission of the referee during a game.

(*3*) Any player for a singles match, or any team for a doubles match, fails to report to play. Normally, 20 minutes from the scheduled game time will be allowed before forfeiture. The tournament chairman may permit a longer delay if circumstances warrant such a decision.

(*4*) If both players for a singles, or both teams for doubles, fail to appear to play for consolation matches or other playoffs, they shall forfeit their ratings for future tournaments and forfeit any trophies, medals, awards, or prize money.

(*5*) [A third technical foul is assessed to any one player or team during the course of a match.]

e. *Referee's Technical.* The referee is empowered, after giving due warning, to deduct one point from a contestant's or his team's total score when in the referee's sole judgment the contestant during the course of the match is being overtly and deliberately abusive beyond a point of reason. The warning referred to will be called a "technical warning" and the actual invoking of this penalty is called a "referee's technical." If, after the technical is called against the abusing contestant and the play is not immediately continued within the allotted time provided for under the existing rules, the referee is empowered to forfeit the match in favor of the abusing contestant's opponent or opponents, as the case may be. The "referee's technical" can be invoked by the referee as many times during the course of a match as he deems necessary.

Rule 3.6 *Scorers.* The scorer shall keep a record of the progress of the game in the manner prescribed by the committee or chairman. As a minimum the progress record shall include the order of serves, outs, and points. The referee or scorer shall announce the score before each serve.

Rule 3.7 *Record Keepers.* In addition to the scorer, the committee may designate additional persons to keep more detailed records for statistical purposes of the progress of the game.

Rule 3.8 *Linesmen.* In any USRA- or NRC-sanctioned tournament match, linesmen may be designated in order to help decide appealed rulings. Two linesmen will be designated by the tournament chairman, and shall at the referee's signal either agree or disagree with the referee's ruling.

The official signal by a linesman to show agreement with the referee is "thumbs up." The official signal to show disagreement is "thumbs down." The official signal for no opinion is an "open palm down."

Both linesmen must disagree with the referee in order to reverse his ruling. If one linesman agrees and one linesman disagrees or has no opinion, the referee's call shall stand.

Rule 3.9 *Appeals.* In any USRA- or NRC-sanctioned tournament match using linesmen, a player or team may appeal certain calls by the referee. These calls are (*1*) kill shots (whether good or bad); (*2*) short serves; and (*3*) double-bounce pickups. At no time may a player or team appeal hinder, avoidable hinder, or technical-foul calls.

The appeal must be directed to the referee, who will then request opinions from the linesmen. Any appeal made directly to a linesman by a player or team will be considered null and void, and forfeit any appeal rights for that player or team for that particular rally.

a. *Kill-shot Appeals.* If the referee makes a call of "good" on a kill-shot attempt that ends a particular rally, the loser of the rally may appeal the call if he feels the shot was not good. If the appeal is successful and the referee's original call reversed, the player who originally lost the rally is declared winner of the rally and is entitled to every benefit under the rules as such—that is, point and/or service.

If the referee makes a call of "bad" or "skip" on a kill-shot attempt, he has ended the rally. The player against whom the call went has the right to appeal the call, if he feels the shot was good. If the appeal is successful and the referee's original call reversed, the player who originally lost the rally is declared winner of the rally and is entitled to every benefit under the rules as winner of a rally.

b. *Short-serve Appeals.* If the referee makes a call of "short" on a serve that the server felt was good, the server may appeal the call. If his appeal is successful, the server is then entitled to two additional serves.

If the served ball was considered by the referee to be an Ace serve to the crotch of the floor and sidewall and in his opinion there was absolutely no way for the receiver to return the serve, then a point shall be awarded to the server.

If the referee makes a "no call" on a particular serve (therefore making it a legal serve) but either player feels the serve was short, either player may appeal the call at the end of the rally. If the loser of the rally appeals and wins his appeal, then the situation reverts back to the point of service with the call becoming "short." If it was a first service, one more serve attempt is allowed. If the server already had one fault, this second fault would cause a sideout.

c. *Double-bounce pickup appeals.* If the referee makes a call of "two bounces," thereby stopping play, the player against whom the call was made has the right of appeal, if he feels he retrieved the ball legally. If the appeal is upheld, the rally is replayed.

If the referee makes no call on a particular play during the course of a rally in which one player feels his opponent retrieved a ball on two or more bounces, the player feeling this way has the right to appeal. However, since the ball is in play, the player wishing to appeal must clearly motion to the referee and linesmen, thereby alerting them to the exact play that is being appealed. At the same time, the player appealing must continue to retrieve and play the rally.

If the appealing player should win the rally, no appeal is necessary. If he loses the rally, and his appeal is upheld, the call is reversed and the "good" retrieve by his opponent becomes a "double-bounce pickup," making the appealing player the winner of the rally and entitled to all benefits thereof.

Rule 3.10 If at any time during the course of a match the referee is of the opinion that a player or team is deliberately abusing the right of appeal, by either repetitious appeals of obvious rulings, or as a means of unsportsmanlike conduct, the referee shall enforce the technical-foul rule.

PART IV. PLAY REGULATIONS

Rule 4.1 *Serve—Generally.*

a. *Order.* The player or side winning the toss becomes the first server and starts the first game, and the third game, if any.

b. *Start.* Games are started from any place in the service zone. No part of either foot may extend beyond either line of the service zone. Stepping on the line (but not beyond it) is permitted. Server must remain in the service zone until the served ball passes short line. Violations are called "foot faults."

c. *Manner.* A serve is commenced by bouncing the ball to the floor in the service zone, and on the first bounce the ball is struck by the server's racquet so that it hits the front wall and on the rebound hits the floor back on the short line, either with or without touching one of the sidewalls.

d. *Readiness.* Serves shall not be made until the receiving side is ready, or the referee has called "Play ball."

Rule 4.2 *Serve—In Doubles.*

a. *Server.* At the beginning of each game in doubles, each side shall inform the referee of the order of service, which order shall be followed throughout the game. Only the first server serves the first time up and continues to serve first throughout the game. When the first server is out, the side is out. Thereafter both players on each side shall serve until a handout occurs. It is not necessary for the server to alternate serves to their opponents.

b. *Partner's Position.* On each serve, the server's partner shall stand erect with his back to the sidewall and with both feet on the floor within the service box until the served ball passes the short line. Violations are called "foot faults."

Rule 4.3 *Defective Serves.* Defective serves are of three types resulting in penalties as follows:

a. *Dead-ball Serve.* A dead-ball serve results in no penalty and the server is given another serve without canceling a prior illegal serve.

b. *Fault Serve.* Two fault serves result in a handout.

c. *Out Serves.* An out serve results in a handout.

Rule 4.4 *Dead-ball Serves.* Dead-ball serves do not cancel any previous illegal serves. They occur when an otherwise legal serve:

a. *Hits Partner.* Hits the server's partner on the fly on the rebound from the front wall while the server's partner is in the service box. Any serve that touches the floor before hitting the partner in the box is a short.

b. *Screen Balls.* Passes too close to the server or the server's partner to obstruct the view of the returning side. Any serve passing behind the server's partner and the sidewall is an automatic screen.

c. *Court Hinders.* Hits any part of the court that under local rules is a dead ball.

Rule 4.5 *Fault Serves.* The following serves are faults, and any two in succession result in a handout.

a. *Foot Faults.* A foot fault results:

(1) When the server leaves the service zone before the served ball passes the short line.

(2) When the server's partner leaves the service box before the served ball passes the short line.

b. *Short Serve.* A short serve is any served ball that first hits the front wall and on the rebound hits the floor in front of the back edge of the short line either with or without touching one sidewall.

c. *Two-side Serve.* A two-side serve is any ball served that first hits the front wall and on the rebound hits two sidewalls on the fly.

d. *Ceiling Serve.* A ceiling serve is any served ball that touches the ceiling after hitting the front wall either with or without touching one sidewall.

e. *Long Serve.* A long serve is any served ball that first hits the front wall and rebounds to the back wall before touching the floor.

f. *Out-of-court Serve.* Any ball going out of the court on the serve.

Rule 4.6 *Out Serves.* Any one of the following serves results in a hand-out:

a. *Bounces.* Bouncing the ball more than three times while in the service zone before striking the ball. A bounce is a drop or throw to the floor, followed by a catch. The ball may not be bounced anywhere but on the floor within the serve zone. Accidental dropping of the ball counts as one bounce.

b. *Missed Ball.* Any attempt to strike the ball on the first bounce that results either in a total miss or in touching any part of the server's body other than his racquet.

c. *Nonfront Serve.* Any served ball that strikes the server's partner, or the ceiling, floor, or sidewall, before striking the front wall.

d. *Touched Serve.* Any served ball that on the rebound from the front wall touches the server, or touches the server's partner while any part of his body is out of the service box, or the server's partner intentionally catches the served ball on the fly.

e. *Out-of-order Serve.* In doubles, when either partner serves out of order.

f. *Crotch Serve.* If the served ball hits the crotch in the front wall it is considered the same as hitting the floor and is an out. A crotch serve into the back wall is good and in play. [A served ball hitting the front-wall sidewall crotch is an out serve.]

Rule 4.7 *Return of Serve.*

a. *Receiving Position.* The receiver or receivers must stand at least 5 feet back of the short line, as indicated by the 3-inch vertical line on each sidewall, and cannot return the ball until it passes the short line. Any infraction results in a point for the server.

b. *Defective Serve.* To eliminate any misunderstanding, the receiving side should not catch or touch a defectively served ball until called by the referee or it has touched the floor the second time.

c. *Fly Return.* In making a fly return the receiver must end up with both feet back of the service zone. A violation by a receiver results in a point for the server.

d. *Legal Return.* After the ball is legally served, one of the players on the receiving side must strike the ball with his racquet either on the fly or after the first bounce and before the ball touches the floor the second time to return the ball to the front wall either directly or after touching one or both sidewalls, the back wall, or the ceiling, or any combination of those surfaces. A returned ball may not touch the floor before touching the front wall. It is legal to return the ball by striking the ball into the back wall first, then hitting the front wall on the fly or after hitting the sidewall or ceiling.

e. *Failure to Return.* The failure to return a serve results in a point for the server.

Rule 4.8 *Changes of Serve.*

a. *Handout.* A server is entitled to continue serving until:

   (1) *Out Serve.* He makes an out serve under Rule 4.6, or

(2) Fault Serves. He makes two fault serves in succession under Rule 4.5, or

(3) Hits Partner. He hits his partner with an attempted return before the ball touches the floor the second time, or

(4) Return Failure. He or his partner fails to keep the ball in play by returning it as required by Rule 4.7(d), or

(5) Avoidable Hinder. He or his partner commits an avoidable hinder under Rule 4.11.

b. *Sideout.* In singles, retiring the server retires the side. In doubles, the side is retired when both partners have been put out, except on the first serve, as provided in Rule 4.2(a).

c. *Effect.* When the server on the side loses the serve, the server or serving side shall become the receiver; and the receiving side, the server; and so alternately in all subsequent services of the game.

Rule 4.9 *Volleys [Rallies].* Each legal return after the serve is called a volley [rally]. Play during volleys [rallies] shall be according to the following rules:

a. *One or Both Hands.* Only the head of the racquet may be used at any time to return the ball. The ball must be hit with the racquet in one or both hands. Switching hands to hit a ball is out. The use of any portion of the body is an out.

b. *One Touch.* In attempting returns, the ball may be touched only once by one player on returning side. [A carry—a ball that rests on his racquet in such a way that the effect is more of a "sling" or "throw" than a hit—is used.] In doubles both partners may swing at, but only one may hit, the ball. Each violation of (a) or (b) results in a handout or point.

c. *Return Attempts.*

(1) In Singles. In singles if a player swings at but misses the ball in play, the player may repeat his attempts to return the ball until it touches the floor the second time.

(2) In Doubles. In doubles, if one player swings at but misses the ball, both he and his partner may make further attempts to return the ball until it touches the floor the second time. Both partners on a side are entitled to an attempt to return the ball.

(3) Hinders. In singles or doubles, if a player swings at but misses the ball in play, and in his or his partner's attempt again to play the ball there is an unintentional interference by an opponent, it shall be a hinder. See Rule 4.10.

d. *Touching Ball.* Except as provided in Rule 4.10(a) (2), any touching of a ball before it touches the floor the second time by a player other than the one making a return is a point or out against the offending player.

e. *Out of-court ball.*

(1) After Return. Any ball returned to the front wall that on the rebound or on the first bounce goes into the gallery or through any opening in a sidewall shall be declared dead and the serve replayed.

(2) No Return. Any ball not returned to the front wall, but that

caroms off a player's racquet into the gallery or into any opening in a sidewall either with or without touching the ceiling, sidewall, or back wall, shall be an out or point against the players failing to make the return.

f. *Dry Ball.* During the game and particularly on service every effort should be made to keep the ball dry. Deliberately wetting shall result in an out. The ball may be inspected by the referee at any time during a game.

g. *Broken Ball.* If there is any suspicion that a ball has broken on the serve or during a volley, play shall continue until the end of the volley. The referee or any player may request that the ball be examined. If the referee decides the ball is broken or otherwise defective, a new ball shall be put into play and the point replayed.

h. *Play Stoppage.*

(1) If a player loses a shoe or other equipment, or foreign objects enter the court, or any other outside interference occurs, the referee shall stop the play.

(2) If a player loses control of his racquet, time should be called after the point has been decided, providing the racquet does not strike an opponent or interfere with ensuing play.

Rule 4.10 *Dead-ball Hinders.* Hinders are of two types—"dead ball" and "avoidable." Dead-ball hinders, described in this rule, result in the point being replayed. Avoidable hinders are described in Rule 4.11.

a. *Situations.* When called by the referee, the following are dead-ball hinders:

(1) *Court Hinders.* Hits any part of the court that under local rules is a dead ball.

(2) *Hitting Opponent.* Any returned ball that touches an opponent on the fly before it returns to the front wall.

(3) *Body Contact.* Any body contact with an opponent that interferes with seeing or returning the ball.

(4) *Screen Ball.* Any ball rebounding from the front wall close to the body of a player on the side that just returned the ball, to interfere with or prevent the returning side from seeing the ball. See Rule 4.4(b).

(5) *Straddle Ball.* A ball passing between the legs of a player on the side that just returned the ball, if there is no fair chance to see or return the ball.

(6) *Other Interference.* Any other unintentional interference that prevents an opponent from having a fair chance to see or return the ball.

b. *Effect.* A call by the referee of a "hinder" stops the play and voids any situation following, such as the ball hitting a player. No player is authorized to call a hinder except on the backswing, and such a call must be made immediately as provided in Rule 3.5(b).

c. *Avoidance.* While making an attempt to return the ball, a player is entitled to a fair chance to see and return the ball. It is the duty of the side that has just served or returned the ball to move so that the receiving side may go straight to the ball and not be required to go around an opponent. The referee should be liberal in calling hinders to discourage any practice of playing the ball where an adversary cannot see it until too late. It is no excuse that the ball is "killed," unless in the opinion of the referee he couldn't return the ball. Hinders should be called without a claim by the player, especially in close plays and on game points.

d. *In Doubles*. In doubles, both players on a side are entitled to a fair and unobstructed chance at the ball, and either one is entitled to a hinder even though it naturally would be his partner's ball and even though his partner may have attempted to play the ball or may have already missed it. It is not a hinder when one player hinders his partner.

Rule 4.11 *Avoidable Hinders*. An avoidable hinder results in an "out" or a point depending upon whether the offender was serving or receiving.

a. *Failure to Move*. Does not move sufficiently to allow opponent his shot.

b. *Blocking*. Moves into a position to effect a block, on the opponent about to return the ball, or, in doubles, one partner moves in front of an opponent as his partner is returning the ball.

c. *Moving into Ball*. Moves in the way and is struck by the ball just played by his opponent.

d. *Pushing*. Deliberately pushing or shoving an opponent during a volley.

Rule 4.12 *Rest Periods*.

a. *Delays*. Deliberate delay exceeding ten seconds by server or receiver shall result in an out or point against the offender.

b. *During Game*. During a game each player in singles, or each side in doubles, either while serving or receiving, may request a "time-out" for a towel, wiping glasses, change, or adjustment. Each "time-out" shall not exceed 30 seconds. No more than three "time-outs" in a game shall be granted each singles player or each team in doubles.

c. *Injury*. No time-out shall be charged to a player who is injured during play. An injured player shall not be allowed more than a total of 15 minutes of rest. If the injured player is not able to resume play after total rests of 15 minutes the match shall be awarded to the opponent or opponents. On any further injury to the same player, the commissioner, if present, or committee, after considering any available medical opinion, shall determine whether the injured player will be allowed to continue.

d. *Between Games*. A five-minute rest period is allowed between the first and second games and a 10-minute rest period between the second and third games. Players may leave the court between games, but must be on the court and ready to play at the expiration of the rest period.

e. *Postponed Games*. Any games postponed by referee due to weather elements shall be resumed with the same score as when postponed.

Rule 5.1 *Draws.* The seeding method of drawing shall be the standard method approved by the USRA and the NRC. All draws in professional brackets shall be the responsibility of the national director of the NRC.

Rule 5.2 *Scheduling.*

a. *Preliminary Matches.* If one or more contestants are entered in both singles and doubles, they may be required to play both singles and doubles on the same day or night with little rest between matches. This is a risk assumed on entering both singles and doubles. If possible the schedule should provide at least a one-hour rest period between all matches.

b. *Final Matches.* Where one or more players have reached the finals in both singles and doubles, it is recommended that the doubles match be played on the day preceding the singles. This would assume more rest between the final matches. If both final matches must be played on the same day or night, the following procedure shall be followed:

(*1*) The singles match be played first.

(*2*) A rest period of not less than ONE HOUR be allowed between the finals in singles and doubles.

Rule 5.3 *Notice of Matches.* After the first round of matches, it is the responsibility of each player to check the posted schedules to determine the time and place of each subsequent match. If any change is made in the schedule after posting, it shall be the duty of the committee or chairman to notify the players of the change.

Rule 5.4 *Third Place.* In championship tournaments: national, state, district, etc. [if there is a playoff for third place], the loser in the semifinals must play for third place or lose his ranking for the next year unless he is unable to compete because of injury or illness. See Rule 3.5 (d) (4).

Rule 5.5 *USRA Regional Tournaments.* Each year the United States and Canada are divided into regions for the purpose of sectional competition preceding the national championships. The exact boundaries of each region are dependent on the location of the regional tournaments. Such locations are announced in *National Racquetball* magazine.

a. Only players residing in the area defined can participate in a regional tournament.

b. Players can participate in only one event in a regional tournament.

c. Winners of open singles in regional tournaments will receive round-trip air coach tickets to the USRA national tourney. Remuneration will be made after arrival at the nationals.

d. A USRA officer will be in attendance at each regional tournament and will co-ordinate with the host chairman.

Awards: No individual award in USRA-sanctioned tournaments should exceed value of more than $25.

Tournament Management: In all USRA-sanctioned tournaments the tournament chairman and/or the national USRA official in attendance may decide on a change of courts after the completion of any tournament game if such a change will accommodate better spectator conditions.

Tournament Conduct: In all USRA-sanctioned tournaments the referee is empowered to default a match if an individual player or team conducts itself to the detriment of the tournament and the game.

Professional Definition: Any player who has accepted $200 or more in prizes and/or prize money in the most recent 12 calendar months is considered a professional racquetball player and ineligible for participation in an USRA-sanctioned tournament bracket.

Amateur Definition: We hold as eligible for amateur racquetball tournaments sanctioned by the USRA anyone except those who qualify as professionals under current USRA-NRC rules.

Pick-a-partner: The essence of the "players' fraternity" has been to allow players to come to tournaments and select a partner, if necessary, regardless of what organization or city he might represent.

Age Brackets: The following age brackets, determined by the age of the player on the first day of the tournament, are:
 Open: Any age can compete.
 Juniors: 18 and under.
 Seniors: 35 and over.
 Masters: 45 and over.
 Golden Masters: 55 and over.
 In doubles both players must be within the specified age bracket.

Basically racquetball rules for one-wall, three-wall, and four-wall are the same, with the following exceptions:

One-wall and Three-wall Rules

One-wall *Court Size* Wall shall be 20 feet in width and 16 feet high, floor 20 feet in width and 34 feet from the wall to back edge of the long line. There should be a minimum of 3 feet beyond the long line and 6 feet outside each sideline. There should be a minimum of 6 feet outside each sideline and behind the long line to permit movement area for the players.

Short Line *Back edge 16 feet from the wall. Service Markers* Lines at least 6 inches long parallel to and midway between the long and short lines, extending in from the sidelines. The imaginary extensions and joining of these lines indicate the service line. Lines are 1½ inches in width. Service Zone—floor area inside and including the short side and service lines. Receiving Zone—floor area in back of short line bounded by and including the long lines and sidelines.

Three-wall *Serve* A serve that goes beyond the sidewalls on the fly is player out or sideout. A serve that goes beyond the long line on a fly but within the sidewall is the same as a "short."